Copyright @2021 by James Bailiff

All rights reserved. No part of this book may be reproduced in any form or by any electronic or mechanical means, including information storage and retrieval systems, without permission in writing from the publisher, except by reviewers, who may quote brief passages in a review.

This publication contains the opinions and ideas of its author. It is intended to provide helpful and informative material on the subjects addressed in the publication. The author and publisher specifically disclaim all responsibility for any liability, loss or risk, personal or otherwise, which is incurred as a consequence, directly or indirectly, of the use and application of any of the contents of this book.

WORKBOOK PRESS LLC
187 E Warm Springs Rd,
Suite B285, Las Vegas, NV 89119, USA

Website:	https://workbookpress.com/
Hotline:	1-888-818-4856
Email:	admin@workbookpress.com

Ordering Information:
Quantity sales. Special discounts are available on quantity purchases by corporations, associations, and others.
For details, contact the publisher at the address above.

ISBN-13:	978-1-953839-71-8 (Paperback Version)
	978-1-953839-72-5 (Digital Version)
REV. DATE:	04/01/2021

JOURNEYING FORWARD TOWARD SPIRITUAL FREEDOM

James D. Bailiff, Author

OUTLINE

Dedication.. i

Preface... ii - vii

Chapter 1:

The Early Years...1-22

Chapter 2:

A Fresh Approach to Faithful Living.................23-54

Chapter 3:

Some implications of the Loving Lifestyle.......55-114

Conclusion..115-120

Notes..121-122

Response Recording Form...................................123

Journeying Forward Toward Spiritual Freedom

DEDICATION

**Dedicated to My
Beloved Brother, Eddie G. Bailiff**

James Bailiff
PREFACE

Occasionally, those who observe our culture are able to sense significant shifts in what has been the norm. For some time, as a person of faith, I have been observing institutional religion, a cultural subset, noticing that it has remained relatively stable during the decades of the 1950's – 1980's. Near the end of that period, significant changes began to occur summed up in one word, *decline*; reflected in reduced participation in important expressions of healthy church life such as attendance at services of corporate worship, Sunday school, Bible study programs and in overall membership decline.

One may look at this trend and conclude that people are losing interest in God and spirituality in general, but this does not seem to be the case. Polls continue to show a widespread interest in things spiritual and for the fulfillment they offer. However, this spiritual interest seems not to be searching for fulfillment in traditional institutional settings, as implied in a statement one often hears these days: "I am *spiritual* but not *religious*."

So, it appears that what we have, occurring all around us, is a decline in institutional religion's influence while, at the same time, a significantly growing interest in spirituality. At first glance, one is tempted to see this as a contradiction. I am convinced it is not. Why? In large part, because my research reveals that a new definition of "religion" has emerged which has influenced our evaluation of its effectiveness. It views religion primarily as a system of beliefs that calls for compliance. This development, in effect, morphs religion into a system that focuses upon the *intellectual* dimension of human beings not upon the *heart*. In other words, with this changed definition of religion, a reference to one's faith is construed to relate to what doctrines one believes and/or to which faith group one belongs. This marks a large move away from the biblical meaning of faith as "trust;" thus an important switch from "experience" to intellectual affirmations. This suggests that the decline we are observing represents a reducing interest in religion as a system of beliefs to be affirmed (an intellectual exercise), along with the erection of a checklist of beliefs, a move that draws clear lines of definition for those who are "in" and those who are "out."

In our review of some surveys that confirm this description, we will discover specific reasons given by survey responders regarding how the development described above has turned them off to institutional religion.

"Spirituality," as understood and practiced by many of our contemporaries, seems less dependent on doctrines, rules and regulations. Its quest places more emphasis upon *experience*, *imagination*, *inclusion* and *flexibility*. Those to whom spirituality is appealing seem to believe that there are more effective settings and ways of experiencing spiritual fulfillment than those offered by institutional religion. If this is so, it would indicate that institutional religion, which in our culture's history has played an important and influential role, is now fading as an effective agent of spiritual fulfillment for many.

From my perspective, it seems that this contemporary dichotomy between "religion" and "spirituality" borders on exaggeration. In this book, we examine the original meaning of "religion." This process suggests that the original meaning of the word is very closely associated with what many of our contemporaries mean by the term "spirituality."

Some contemporary scholars have been helpful by focusing directly upon the relationship between the two terms; particularly Diana Butler Bass' thinking and research reflected in her 2012 book, *Christianity After Religion* where she acknowledges that there is a way in which the two can serve and complement one another, e.g., institutional religion can learn to become more spiritual and spirituality can become more meaningfully structured.I can testify that, particularly in recent years, in my own experience of following Christ from and through an institutional base, I have made adjustments that represent the complementarity of "religion" and "spirituality." For example, while I find the usefulness of church doctrine to give definition and clarity to my faith, at the same time, the doctrines I find to be helpful are those that lead me to deeper spiritual experience and to more significant activity on the part of restorative/reconciling justice and mercy. To say it another way: My involvement with the church as a community of faith continues to be meaningful and, in some very genuine ways, fulfilling. At the same time, what I find meaningful has undergone significant change. My approach to living out the faith has been substantially altered. The meaning of "religion" has shifted in some important ways. Yet, unlike the folk who declare themselves to be spiritual but not religious, I describe myself as both religious and spiritual. Thus, I discuss the meaning of "religion" in its earlier sense, before the emergence of its newer definition and how, in that sense, its goals are very similar to the goals of "spirituality" as that term is understood in contemporary culture.

In my view the newer definition of religion as a system of beliefs with attending rules and regulations has affected the shape of institutional religion in significantly negative ways, changing the meaning, shape, and goals of religion in ways that reduce its appeal as a fulfilling way of life in our complex world. Indeed, one of the forces motivating me to write this book is my own experience of irrelevance with some of the institution's theology, methodology, interests, and even doctrines. There have occurred shifts in my thinking and action, regarding what I consider to be the priorities of following Jesus Christ.

The title of this book, *Journeying Forward toward Spiritual Freedom*, implies a yearning for freedom to test new ways of looking at spiritual issues, new methods for experiencing God and the natural world, a freedom that many used-to-be church folk found lacking in their experience with institutional religion.

Apparently, this perceived journey into the freedom of spirituality is growing in popularity these days as more people seem to be joining it. In some important ways, it is a journey for me as well, and, perhaps, for you.

What does this journey toward freedom mean? What are its implications for the Church? For society in general? Its meaning and the implications thereof are the focus of this book which begins, in Chapter 1, with an account of the early years of my own journey. From there, in Chapter 2, I highlight an experience in the ministry of Jesus; particularly one of his core teachings that I consider to be a paradigm for changing the focus of religion and spiritualty which, initially, makes Jesus appear to be anti-religious.

Chapter 3 becomes what I think of as the ice cream and cake portion of the work in which we explore some of the remarkable results that grow out of following one's faith and heart in fresh new directions to which Jesus invites us.

Journeying Forward Toward Spiritual Freedom

You may find some of this work challenging and disturbing. It is not designed to encourage us who are comfortable with a non-critical perspective, who feel that "old timey" formulations are sufficient to fulfill and make us effective in this new day with its increased pluralism and diversity. On the other hand, you may find here some inspiration to explore new ways of relating to God and to others. You may experience a combination of disturbance and inspiration as you read. Whatever your response, I trust that you will be as open and patient with me as you can and that you will still be accepting if you consider me to be off base.

Finally, much of this book relates to my personal journey. I very much appreciate your sharing it with me. As I have indicated, I suspect that some, if not many, of my readers may find themselves on a similar journey. That thought pleases me considerably.

At the end of the book you will find a chapter-b-by-chapter form on which to record thoughts, impressions, etc. for further exploration, reflection, and group discussion. Feel free to use it as you wish.

Thank you for your interest.

Jim Bailiff

October 21, 2020

CHAPTER 1

The Early Years

"When someone tells me that he has never had a moment of probing religious doubt I find myself wondering whether he has ever known a moment of vital religious conviction." --Harold Bosley

"There lives more faith in honest doubt, believe me, than in half the creeds."

--Alfred Lord Tennyson

I remember well those years of my early adolescence in the village of Heaton, North Carolina. It was the late 1940s and I would not let myself miss the informal "show" going on around the pot-bellied stove at Uncle Jim's store. It was on that spot that the older men would gather on Saturday mornings to discuss, of all things, politics and religion. It was their discussions about religion that captured my attention. Among the topics of their discussions were these: Is Hell a literal place of fire? How long does that torture last? Which of the several religious denominations is most right? Must one be a member of a church in order to be in good standing with God? Is baptism essential for salvation? What form of baptism is the right one? How often should a congregation observe the Lord's Supper? Who is welcomed at the Table of Communion? Is the Pope the antichrist? Does the Bible prophesy the coming of the automobile? What about Christ's second coming? From the signs of the time, can we predict its nearness?

I'm sure these were not all the issues discussed, but they are the ones I most remember. The old sages were rarely in agreement on their answers to such questions. Sometimes, more heat than light was created as various ones disagreed vehemently. Often the disagreements were so severe, or the loss of an argument so painful, I thought some may be offended to the point of not returning for future gatherings. But when the next Saturday morning rolled around, there they were sitting around the stove on nail kegs, cocked and ready to fire their opinions about what they perceived to be the most important questions facing humankind.

Among those Saturday morning "nail keg theologians" were some of the leaders of the church I attended. I knew them well from my involvement there. At this time—early in my adolescence—I found considerable meaning in its worship, fellowship, and call to service.

I was just beginning to develop the critical thinking that accompanies any healthy journey. Though I respected my congregational leaders who shared in these discussions, secretly I had begun to feel that many of their subjects—particularly the manner in which they were discussed—not only seemed insensitive to the thought that God loves all creation, but also seemed to be irrelevant to the experience of everyday living.

Surely, I concluded, there has got to be more to Christian Faith than a preoccupation with issues that seem to be out of touch, not only with the spirit of Jesus, but with what is really needed in a world caught up in its second World War, along with the lasting results of the Great Depression; particularly in Appalachia. Moreover, I felt that the group's mood and agenda severely restricted the freedom to think critically, to dream and hope about the future.

Quite to my surprise I was beginning to suspect that religion, as I was hearing about and witnessing its effects upon members of the Saturday group, was more restrictive than freeing. While I was aware that God loved me and wanted me to be whole and healthy, I was not able to understand my sense that, at the same time, my religion was attempting to put me into both a physical and mental straight jacket and to dwarf my thinking and behavior. Much of what I would later recognize as bad theology did not fit into my perception of what was whole and healthy for body and mind. At that point in my life I was not sophisticated enough to understand that the mixed feelings between my personal faith and the seemingly irrelevant theology expressed in those Saturday morning discussions represented the early stages of a journey that I continue to this very day—a search for the core truth of Christian Faith as opposed to peripheral or incompatible matters. Though somewhat frustrated with my ambivalence, I continued to find meaning in my own relationship to Christ and to the Church. Corporate worship continued to inspire, Sunday school's religious education continued to stimulate important questions and to point out a direction for further exploration, fellowship with my adolescent peers and, especially, with "grownups" whose love for me was very clear, continued to give my life meaning and direction. But, while I was finding meaning in all these expressions of discipleship, I was becoming increasingly aware that there were so-called religious subjects being addressed that were not inspiring, and positions taken on these subjects which felt tedious and unfulfilling.

As my journey continued, the church and its faith became an increasingly large part of my life. I became concerned about adolescent friends who appeared to be skating on thin ice as they dabbled with tobacco, alcohol and sex. Little did I understand that during adolescence such experimentation may not be unnatural.

Though I felt I was able to weigh religious issues and ideas and make judgments about what fit my mind and spirit and what did not, I now see that I was dangerously close to falling into the quagmire of moralistic judgmentalism with its tendency to condemn the questionable activity of others. On reflection, it seems as though my ability to identify and critique irrelevant theology (a strength) was neutralized by my vulnerability to judge and condemn what appeared to me as sinful behavior (a weakness).

In spite of it all, my journey in faith continued. Eventually I reached the point of feeling called into full-time Christian service and preparation for ordination to pastoral ministry. Though the call to ministry would come to me as a sophomore in high school, it would go underground for a period of about three years as I explored other vocational options. But by the middle of my first year in college the call broke forth from its underground hiding place, erupting into full awareness that, more than anything, I wanted to begin preparation for ministry and to spend my life as a pastor.

So, the years of intentional preparation began in college. Mid-year, I transferred from my state university into what was then known as Johnson Bible College, arriving on campus late one evening to check into my dorm and get ready for classes the next day.

Soon I realized that I had entered a world quite different from that of the university. The campus was considerably smaller, the students fewer. Professors were more personal, aided by class sizes that were much more manageable than those

I had known in the university. I noted, too, that the curriculum was more sharply focused upon Greek, biblical studies, church history, theology, and pastoral counseling. Yet, of course, there were other important curriculum requirements which focused upon the arts and sciences.

At Johnson I dove into my studies head first, rarely coming up for air. Immersed in them I had little social life, feeling that I had already lost a year and that I must compensate by giving my all. In some cases, the quality of my professors exceeded anything I had experienced at the university. In other cases, I experienced them as inferior. Overall, I was pleased with the quality of my new educational environment.

Sometime during my second full year at Johnson, I began to experience an intensification in my critical perspective. It was of the same flavor as that which I had known when critiquing the Saturday morning group of my early adolescence, a penchant for *evaluating* what I was seeing and hearing.

The general atmosphere at the college was theologically conservative, bordering on fundamentalism. For example, the Bible was considered to be the literal written word of God which held vast treasures for those who studied it. Doctrines, especially the distinctive doctrines of our denominational tradition, were held to be sacrosanct. The institutional church was viewed as the Body of Christ within which one must find oneself in order to be right with God. Theology was understood as intellectual reflection upon Scripture and dogma, both of which were perceived as having come to humanity as God's direct revelation. The work of theology, therefore, was oriented to the past. Its task was to interpret the already completed revelation, requiring a first-century mindset that resisted a theologically critical perspective. Moreover, because it was so focused upon truth as an objective set of sacred revelation and dogma from the past, it lacked a present and future dimension. I sensed their perception that affirming those dimensions would imply that such theological reflection was inherently dynamic which, in turn, would suggest the existence of truth, beyond what had already been revealed, truth yet to be discovered. Such implications, I sensed, possessed a distinct threat to the conservative mindset of my teachers and many of my fellow students.

Some professors were excellent in helping us to understand biblical content and making application of it. My homiletics (the art of preaching) professor, Fred Craddock, was superbly gifted in helping us develop the ability to formulate sermons that were faithful to scripture and, at the same time, relevant to our hearers.

Generally, Johnson's culture left the impression that, though it was an undergraduate program, it was of such quality that one did not need to proceed to seminary. It was not unusual to hear the Dean of the school state that clearly.

By my senior year I was aware that I had not received adequate exposure to the wider scholarly world of biblical and systematic theology. While I felt that I was receiving a good education in the original biblical languages, the content of biblical stories, the art of preaching, pastoral counseling, and some aspects of church history, I felt something was missing.

My extra-curricular reading had given me exposure to some world class biblical and systematic theologians—Karl Barth, Reinhold Niebuhr, Paul Tillich, *et.al*. I learned from reading them that biblical scholarship consisted of more than learning the *content* of the Bible, important as that is. I sensed that I needed, also, to understand how and when various books of the Bible came about and the cultural influences that gave them birth. In short, I had not been introduced to the nature and methods of *higher criticism* which had emerged in respected theological centers of Europe and held large sway in those of the United States. This movement was a reasoned, scholarly and scientific method of approaching the nature of Scripture. With its emphasis upon the dynamic nature of Christian Faith, it expanded the scope of theological focus while, at the same time, freeing it from the myopic perception that its sole task was to interpret the message contained in revealed

Scripture and Dogma.

As I continued my extra-curricular reading, I began to realize that I had never questioned the traditional position that Moses was the writer of the first five books of the Bible—Genesis, Exodus, Leviticus, Numbers and Deuteronomy. I had not learned that these five books are most likely the products of a process in which several "ancient editors" examined the numerous, clearly discernable, strands of oral tradition and wove them into the final book forms we now have in the Pentateuch. I had not learned in Bible College that of the three synoptic gospels—Matthew, Mark and Luke—Mark was written first (just beyond the middle of the first century) and that Matthew and Luke relied heavily upon Mark's work in the composition of their own renderings. I was not sufficiently aware that the Gospel of John had been written considerably later (very near the end of the first century) when Greek thought had a heightened influence upon the thinking of church leaders. During those college years, I had not learned to measure the impact of modern cosmology upon the three-tiered-universe concept prevalent in biblical times, nor the implications of slight revisions in the cosmologies which emerged prior to the primary revolution spurred by Copernicus. I had not learned, adequately, that the mission of the Church must take seriously *this* world as well as the *next*, and that preaching the gospel has to include in its focus issues of justice, peace, and environmental concerns. I had begun to understand that these developments—which had been largely ignored in my school's curriculum—had considerable implications for biblical studies and theology. At the time, I remember suspecting that my scholastic non-exposure to such important consideration may have been officially intentional. However, further reflection through the years has convinced me that while some of it may have been intentional, the time-frame was one in which such issues were not considered to be of paramount importance for leaders in my denominational tradition.

I reached the point at which I was spending as much time reading beyond Johnson's prescribed curriculum as I was within it, and in searching for those sources in other places than my college library in which they were largely absent. The advent of online accessories had not yet developed, so I had to do manual searches through catalogues and periodicals I found in other places.

In addition to the new insights I was gaining from my reading, I was serving as a student pastor in a small congregation in East Tennessee (the town of Erwin). In many ways that experience was fulfilling, providing me with a "flock" to tend, an arena in which to hone my rudimentary pastoral skills, and, perhaps most importantly, a community of believers with whom to fellowship and practice faith.

All this, however, was in the theological context in

which I had been reared. It was very conservative---perhaps even fundamentalist—with a strong flavor of moralism, dogmatism, and legalism.

What do I mean by those terms? By *moralism* I mean an excessive concern for personal morality; often based upon questionable standards and possessing a tendency to consider much human activity to be sinful which, in turn, compels its practitioners toward condemnation of the offenders. For example, moralism often condemns any use of alcohol consumption with no consideration given to the appropriateness of moderation. Among those who practice moralism there is very deep concern for the kind of movies one sees or the literature one reads. Even great literature or art that speaks of or displays sexual activity is suspect.

My precious mother, who was a moralist to the core, refused to let me spend the night with my favorite cousin, Stewart, because, as she put it, "he and his brother play Monopoly in which gaming die, like those in gambling venues, are used."

By *dogmatism* I mean reliance upon a system of doctrines thought to be equivalent to absolute truth and often considered to be more important than the needs of people. For example, the belief that on Sunday one should not go shopping or do other mundane things because that day is reserved for "holy" activity. Then there is the belief that Jesus' divinity is derived solely from the doctrine of the virgin birth or that the only valid baptism is that done by total immersion. But the most telling characteristic of dogmatism is its implication that faith is, essentially, a system of beliefs which demands our compliance, often by surrendering our capacity for practical reasoning.

Then there is *legalism* by which I mean the perception that our relationship with God is primarily a legal one and that our responsibility is to identify the laws of God and to obey them. Good performance in that obedience brings us into a right relationship with God. And, if our religious tradition is the least bit sectarian, such legalism not only puts us right with God but provides us the ammunition with which to do battle with other religious folk who, in our perception, follow *false* doctrines or practices.

I encountered a large dose of legalism in my student congregation. For example, I remember being called into question for playing football on a Sunday afternoon (after church!!). And I'll never forget the baptism of a young lady which occurred during a Sunday morning worship service. The baptismal pool was filled and, in white robes, she and I descended into the water for an occasion of full immersion. After the baptism, when it was discovered by those assisting the young woman that some of the hair on top of her head was not wet, an elder came rushing to me, exclaiming, "Pastor, you must baptize her again, she is not totally wet!" As diplomatically as I could at the moment, I replied, "I consider her to be baptized and do not intend a do over!"

When I encountered a considerable amount of moralism, dogmatism, and legalism in my student congregation, immediately I was able to recognize it. It brought back echoes of extreme forms of it practiced by my home pastor during my high school years. He was always harping on the character flaws of parishioners and community leaders, both from the pulpit and in group discussions. In addition, he felt, along with many of his colleagues in what was called the Restoration Movement, that our particular denomination was divinely charged to restore "New Testament Christianity." For example, his stated goal was to restore the way in which the local church in the New Testament was organized—autonomous and independent—and to restore a non-denominational name (our congregation was called "The Church at Heaton" although there were other churches in and around the village.) Communion was to be celebrated/observed every Sunday and baptism was defined exclusively as adult baptism, always to be done by full immersion in water.

Little did the pastor seem to recognize that in the New Testament Church there were diverse forms of church structure and of practices such as Holy Communion. He manifested no recognition of the different concepts held by Peter and James in the

Jerusalem church and Paul in Israel's outlying areas and Asia Minor. He, as well as the denominational tradition of which he was a part, was simply naïve about the complexities of the New Testament Church which reflected no single organizational model or set of beliefs that could be simply copied 20 centuries later.

While my college community was less saturated with the above "isms" than those I encountered in my home church and my student congregation, its very conservative stance nurtured an environment in which they could thrive, largely unchallenged. On reflection, I am most disappointed that the college did not better prepare its students to identify and confront these forces they would encounter in their parishes. (Now, forty years later, in defense of the college—now Johnson University—I wish to emphasize that it has transitioned well beyond some of the limitations I have identified here and has moved more into the mainstream of theological education with a high percentage of its faculty holding doctorates from some of the world's most prestigious schools.)

Following graduation from Johnson, two things were clear in my mind: (1) I, now, needed a first-class *seminary* education, and (2) I was ready to move beyond the very conservative tradition in which I had spent my first 22 years. I was convinced that I could no longer remain in that denominational tradition with integrity.

While I was—and continue to be—grateful for much that it gave me—a passion for worship, study, service—neither in my heart nor my mind could I find a continuing home there. Home would need to be found elsewhere.

I was aware of my hunger for a setting in which I could practice the implications of God's unconditional and inclusive love, a setting that affirmed diversity as consistent with God's design, and viewed Christian discipleship as being at its best when it was motivated by compassionate love for God and creation, while being intentional about speaking and acting out its faith in appropriate demands for justice and peace. I wanted to be in a setting in which I could be intellectually honest and authentically effective in meeting the needs of society while, at the same time, finding affirmation and acceptance by those who may have reached different conclusions in their journey.

To whom would I now turn? Living in Tennessee I had learned about the excellent reputation of Vanderbilt University's Divinity School and of Dr. Herman Norton who was Dean of the Disciples House and professor of American Church History. But, before turning to Dr. Norton and Vanderbilt, I was aware of some significant challenges to be met: I needed more academic work to prepare for the intellectual rigors of Divinity School; particularly in the field of philosophy. In addition, I had some important work toward closure with persons who remained in my denominational tradition.

To meet the first of those challenges, I enrolled in a degree program at East Tennessee State University with a major focus in philosophy. Since almost all my undergraduate education had been done in Bible College with its distinctive religious culture, I felt a need to study in a setting that was less oriented toward my own tradition. Moreover, my studies at Johnson were steeped in linear, rationalistic thinking in which much of the meaning of the great stories of Scripture were diminished, either by the limitations of the rational, linear process or through acceptance on what some would call "blind faith." I needed exposure to the dynamics of philosophy and to the nature of the phenomenon of religion itself.

In two years, I had completed my degree work at ETSU and felt more prepared to take on the demands of Divinity school but, as indicated, I had some closure work to do with persons in my own denominational tradition. I wanted to begin this important task before diving into the Vanderbilt experience.

By this time, my former pastor had moved on. Though in many ways he was beloved to me, at the same time, I knew he was a clear example of the kind of pastor I did *not* want to be. The new pastor of my home congregation was Dr. Robert Fife, a very open and competent pastor whose fellowship

I had enjoyed in other settings and whom I now considered to be my pastor. At my request he had given me an appointment to discuss where I was in my journey.

I remember the day well. As we met, I poured my heart out to him expressing my disappointment with several aspects of my denominational tradition and making the case that I felt I could no longer serve in it with integrity. He asked several "clarifying" questions, all of which were right on target and enabled me more freely and thoroughly to express my feelings. With a PhD from Indiana University, Dr. Fife was able to identify with my felt need to continue toward seminary. As one whose ministry had been progressive and ecumenical, he understood my discomfort with moralism, dogmatism and legalism. He listened carefully as I spoke of exploring a new tradition in which I could feel more integrity. After a lengthy period, he seemed clearly to understand my journey and my concerns. He looked directly into my eyes with his own special pastoral compassion and said, "Jim, I hear you, not only with my ears, but also with my heart. I believe you are at a very special point in your life. You seem to have thought and prayed it through and I want you to know you have my blessing in continuing your search with Dr. Norton at Vanderbilt. I know him to be a very responsible and upstanding scholar."

As I departed my old denominational tradition,

James Bailiff

I made a prayerful effort to maintain the several friendships I had made with colleagues and acquaintances. Some of those have lasted over the years. As I write, I am prayerfully aware that one of my best and enduring friends from Johnson Bible College, at 86 years of age, is now on a ventilator in North Carolina, struggling for his life.

But not all friendships would survive my departure. One of my dear friends from my student pastor days, who had responded to the call to ministry and became my roommate while at Johnson, was deeply disappointed in my change of denominational traditions.

In an effort to salvage what had been a very deep friendship, I visited him at his home that summer. During our time together I said to him, "When you visit with me, I would love to have you be my pulpit guest on Sunday morning. He responded, "Thanks, I'll be glad to do that, but I cannot return the favor." I was curious to learn the reasoning behind his refusal to return the invitation; so, I pressed for clarification. Finally, he responded, "I cannot invite someone into my pulpit who believes neither in the inspiration of Scripture nor the divinity of Christ." I asked how he had drawn that conclusion about me, for I affirmed both. He responded, "The liberals you have joined don't believe those things and now you are one of them." After sharing with him that I suspected he was responding to a stereotype of 19th century Protestant liberalism which had been largely abandoned, he continued to insist that my presumed unorthodoxy disqualified me from preaching in his church.

Though I have not given up either my love for him or my effort at reconciliation, our relationship continues to be strained. He has deep sincerity (which I respect) but I consider him to be a prisoner of the "isms" which will continue to restrict his support of diversity of thought and practice. With such rigidity I do have difficulty and find myself struggling to prevent falling into the trap of being intolerant of those who are intolerant.

My Vanderbilt experience turned out to be splendid! Directed by outstanding professors like Gordon Kaufman, Jack Forstman and Walter Harrelson in Theology, Phillip Hyatt and Leander Keck in Biblical Studies, Liston Mills in Pastoral Care and Counseling, Herman Norton and Gregory Armstrong in Church History, I felt I was swimming in refreshing waters which in many ways represented a rebirth for me both in terms of the mind and the spirit.

That experience would be followed 10 years later by earning my Doctor of Ministry degree from Emory University's Candler School of Theology. With the deepening of my pastoral experience in those 10 intervening years I was able to identify and focus upon areas I felt would be most beneficial in the practice of ministry. Influenced by the likes of Emory's Quinten Hand and Theodore Jennings, I experienced those years of study as transformative.

In the process of my continuing education, beginning with Vanderbilt, I found a home in a new denominational setting where I was welcomed and in which I found deep faithfulness along with considerably more theological flexibility and diversity. All that felt, and continues to feel, good to me. But, even in the new setting I continued to encounter a measure of the "isms" described earlier. These were much less forceful and energetic in my new setting, but I continued to be impressed with the role played by dogmatism and legalism among Christian folk. Dogma continues to play a strong role in the church, although it is less forceful and rigid that what I had previously known. Legalism and moralism can still be found among followers of Christ; particularly when it comes to determining our response to several of the issues with which increasing diversity has confronted us—issues of gender, ethnicity, immigration and the like. And, to my disappointment, I continue to find pockets of resistance to change. Everywhere church folk seem to have a high degree of commitment to the sacred cow of "but we've always done it this way."

In late 1966 theologian Langdon Gilkey delivered a lecture to a group of church leaders, including several seminarians and me, in which he expressed his conviction that one of the major roles for the pastor is that of theologian, one whose spiritual and academic development equips her or him to give spiritual guidance to parishioners who journey through the complexities of modern life.

That lecture left a deep impression on me. It influenced me to renew my commitment to becoming a competent theologian for my people. My calling was not to lecture on theology as in a seminary setting, holding a PhD in one of the specialized fields of formal theology, but to be a trained pastor equipped to stand among my people observing the world around us; seeking, there, to discern God's leading while, at the same time, reaching into our rich faith tradition, coupling both culture and tradition as a way of finding meaning and effectiveness in our practice of the faith to the glory of God and for the good of all. I clearly understood that to accomplish such task I must continuously discipline myself to learning and to weaving the various strands of life into some meaningful tapestry that will inspire and aid those who are on the journey of faith with me.

Therefore, while active in pastoral ministry, I designated and protected times for study, prayer and reflection, defending them from the, sometimes, intensive invasions of other pastoral demands. Now, fifty years later and in retirement, most of my mornings continue to be dedicated to that discipline.

I am constantly impressed with the ways in which perspectives from the biblical story and theological concepts, in dialogue with our ever-changing culture, yield new insights. In my view, it is that character that makes for dynamic faith and spirituality to be *acted out* versus static religion simply to be *believed in*.

Some of my most recent discoveries in this process have been new dimensions of meaning that have grown out of my reflection upon Jesus' "Great Commandment." There he declares what I consider to be an Ethic of Love, i.e., a commitment to loving God with our entire being and to loving our neighbor as we love ourselves. In my serious focus upon the "Great Commandment" and its ethic of love I have discovered new energy that continues to fuel my continuing journey beyond a religious belief system to a spirituality that provides freedom sufficient for discovering new passion for living among the challenges and opportunities of the 21st century.

I invite you now to proceed with me to the next chapter in which we take a close look at Jesus' teaching through the "Great Commandment."

CHAPTER 2
A Fresh Approach to Faithful Living-Discoveries in the Great Commandment

"Be such a man, and live such a life, that if every man were such as you and every life like yours, the earth would be God's Paradise.

--Phillips Brooks

Here is Matthew's rendering of the Great Commandment:

When the Pharisees heard that he (Jesus) had silenced the Sadducees, they gathered together, and one of them, a lawyer, asked him a question to test him. "Teacher, which commandment in the law is the greatest? He said to him, "'You shall love the Lord your God with all your heart, and with all your soul and with all your mind.' This is the greatest and first commandment. And a second is like it, 'You shall love your neighbor as yourself.' On these two commandments hang all the law and the prophets" (Matthew 22:34-40—New Revised Standard Version).

To get at what is going on in this passage it's important for us to understand that Jesus has reached the point in his three-year ministry at which his popularity is perceived as a genuine threat to the religious establishment; particularly to the party called the Pharisees who consider themselves to be the guardians of Israel's faith.

"Who does this new kid on the block think he is?!" they must have thought.

Then, consider what has happened to Judaism by this time in the first century. In short, this once great religious movement which had brought monotheism (God is one) to the land, had also coined the terminology Jesus uses in the passage we are considering ("You shall love the Lord your God....and your neighbor as yourself" See Deuteronomy 6:5 and Leviticus 19:18) In addition, it had a faith that led the Israelites out of Egypt, sustained them for forty years in the wilderness, and empowered them to conquer and inhabit the "Promised Land." Along the way, it had gifted the people with the "Ten Commandments." Now, at this point in the first century, at the time of Jesus ministry, Judaism—particularly Pharisaic Judaism—had become static and stultified, morphing into a corpus of legalism. As modeled by the Pharisees, self-righteousness had become a virtue. You may remember that it was a Pharisee who prayed, God, I thank you that I am not like other people, thieves, rogues, adulterers, or even like this tax collector. I fast twice a week; I give a tenth of all my income" (Luke 18:11b-12—NRSV).

Israel's once dynamic relationship with God had become eroded by religious legalism's codification of 613 religious commands, 248 positive ones corresponding to the number of parts of the body and 365 negative commands corresponding to the days of the year; all of which required obedience if one was to be in a right relationship with God.

The evolution toward this expansion into 613 commands is illustrated by what had been done regarding the fourth of the original Ten Commandment: "You shall remember the Sabbath day and keep it holy." Eventually it was perceived not to be specific enough so, through the machinations of religious legalism, more specific prescriptions and prohibitions were formulated. For example, on the Sabbath, a hungry person, finding eggs baked in the hot sand by the sun could consume them, but he could not prepare a fire to cook them. That action would break the Sabbath law. This type of process developed other commands until the large corpus of religious law had accrued.

To my mind, such legalism perceives the life of faith as a laborious journey, made more difficult by the task of carrying a heavy rule book. When the journey requires a decision, that decision is made by turning to the proper page and rule number to discover the required action.

From the previous chapter you have seen my familiarity with such limitations. I suspect this rulebook approach to religious faith is something with which many of you are familiar as well.

The rules and regulations of Pharisaic Judaism had become so numerous and complex that the Pharisees made use of lawyers to keep them straight. In fact, this passage before us stipulates that the Pharisee who asked Jesus to identify the greatest commandment was himself a lawyer whose intent was to trick Jesus into making a mistake for which the Pharisees could nail him.

Now consider Jesus' response: "'You shall love the Lord your God with all your heart and with all your soul, and with all your mind.' This is the greatest and first commandment. And a second is like it: 'You shall love your neighbor as yourself.' On these two commandments hang all the law and the prophets."

Jesus' response does not shy away from the lawyer's question. He answers it clearly. But the answer is probably much weightier than the Pharisee expected. I imagine they expected Jesus to comb through the pages of 613 commands, place his finger on one of them and declare, "This one!" What Jesus does, however, is to leapfrog back into Hebrew history, to an early precedent, and lift up two commands contained in Deuteronomy and Leviticus.

To my mind, the Pharisee was astounded, first, that Jesus was that well acquainted with the Hebrew faith. After all, was he not just a charismatic itinerant preacher who had risen from the common people of the land?! Perhaps he was more astounded that Jesus had the gall to confront the legalistic system so diplomatically by citing two foundational commands from the Hebrew faith's earlier (and purer) days, while suggesting that "on these two, hang all the law and the prophets."

In my thinking Jesus' response, in effect, circumvents the rule book approach to the life of faith. By doing so, he is showing how far the religious system has strayed from a once vibrant faith. No doubt, this heightened the threat that Jesus already represented to the religious establishment. Now he would be perceived as one who was going to change the definition, nature and course of their religion.

I say all this, realizing that Jesus is a Jew, reared in the faith of Judaism and probably, at this point, is attempting—perhaps somewhat like Martin Luther in the Protestant Reformation—to reform the faith. For Jesus to suggest that the commands to love God and neighbor transcend all the 613 rules and regulations of the establishment and, further, to declare that these two are a valid summation of all the teaching of the religious law and the prophets, must have seemed to the Pharisees to be terribly audacious! It is no wonder that Pharisees were among those who would condemn Jesus and find satisfaction in his eventual crucifixion. Yet, for balance, it is helpful for us to remember that among the Pharisees were those—notably Nicodemus—who saw Jesus' integrity, affirmed his authenticity and responded positively, though cautiously, to his message.

Let's take a closer look at the message Jesus is bringing as it is reflected in his encounter with the lawyer. In my thinking, this passage represents nothing short of a paradigm shift in our thinking about the nature of religion.

The long-held notion that religion is an arrangement in which the exalted God laid down the law to the people and that the people, by obeying that law won God's acceptance, is being challenged by Jesus.

This passage, when related to other incidents recorded in the Gospels, shows Jesus as one who believes God's acceptance already exists, before any attempt to respond is made on our part. In other words, we don't have to *earn* God's acceptance, it is already a *gift* of God's love.

Also shown, is the concept that life's highest duty does not consist of fulfilling the agenda of institutional religion's many doctrines, rules and regulations but lies, rather, in responding to God's call to love.

Could it be that our love responding to God and to others has been God's expectation from the beginning and that the religious establishment's message stepped in and changed things? Could it be that is always God's intention to free us from the burdens religion so often imposes, burdens that make the situation more difficult than it needs to be? Could it be that, both our ancestors and we are so confounded by the profundity of *grace* that we have major difficulty *accepting* the acceptance of God? Could it be that one of the greatest difficulties we have is that of moving beyond our preoccupation with self; thus, making it very difficult to love beyond ourselves?

I believe Jesus is redefining the nature of ethics, calling us from a multifaceted ethic of obedience to a legalistic system of works to an ethic of love and grace. In my thinking Jesus is asking us to give up the rule book mentality—to give it to him and let him discard it. Then we can begin to move forward, realizing that he offers the gift of freedom gushing from the grace-filled heart of God, freedom that has the power to transform us into creatures of love.

Now, as we consider the shift from a rule book mentality to an ethic of love let us reflect upon some crucial questions: Does this move us toward *less* personal responsibility or *more*? Is the directive to live by love *specific enough* to give us adequate guidance in the conduct of our lives? Is it *broad enough* to include all that is deserving of our love?

A concern shared by followers of Jesus from the first century to our own is whether, when we are freed from religious law, we are also freed from responsibility to think and behave ethically.

Let's do a brief review: Remember the Apostle Paul's stated case for freedom from law:

> But now God's way of putting people right with himself has been revealed. *It has nothing to do with law (*italics mine), even though Moses and the prophets gave their witness to it. God puts people right through their faith in Jesus Christ. God does this to all who believe in Christ, because there is no difference at all: everyone has sinned and is far away from God's saving presence. But by the free gift of God's grace all are put right with him through Christ Jesus, who sets them free (Romans 3:21-23—Today's English Version).

Paul's reflections stimulated some interesting reaction. For example, some took this to mean that they could affirm Jesus as Lord and simply conduct their lives as they pleased. Their thinking seemed to run as follows: "Christ puts into a right relationship with God when we trust that God's grace accepts us. Moreover, when we trust that acceptance, we're O.K. Now that we're O.K. with God, we can sow our wild oats and do whatever we want."

Does this line of thinking sound familiar? My sense is that, to some extent, such is often reflected in those who verbally affirm the reality of God's grace. I hasten to suggest that it also represents a distortion of Paul's teaching. So, sensing its presence, the apostle writes: "Should we continue to live in sin so that God's grace will increase? Certainly not! We have died to sin—how can we go on living in it" (Romans 6:1-2—TEV)?

Focusing specifically upon new life in Christ in his *Letter to the Colossians*, Paul pens this more extensive statement:

So, if you have been raised with Christ, seek the things that are above, where Christ is, seated at the right hand of God. Set your minds on things that are above, not on things that are on earth, for you have died and your life is hidden with Christ in God. When Christ who is your life is revealed, then you also will be revealed with him in glory.

Put to death, therefore, whatever in you is earthly: fornication, impurity, passion, evil desire, and greed (which is also idolatry) .... These are the ways you also once followed, when you were living that life. But now you must get rid of all such things—anger, wrath, malice, slander, and abusive language from your mouth. Do not lie to one another, seeing that you have stripped off the old self with its practices, and have clothed yourselves with the new self, which is being renewed in knowledge according to the image of its creator.... As God's chosen ones, holy and beloved, cloth yourselves with compassion, kindness, humility, meekness and patience. Bear with one another and, if anyone has a complaint against another, forgive each other; just as the Lord has forgiven you, so you also must forgive. Above all, clothe yourselves with love, which binds everything together in perfect harmony. And let the peace of Christ rule in your hearts to which indeed you were called in the one body. And be thankful! Let the word of Christ dwell in you richly, teach and admonish one another in all wisdom, and with gratitude in your hearts sing psalms, hymns, and spiritual songs to God. And whatever you do, in word or deed, do everything in the name of the Lord Jesus, giving thanks to God the father through him" (3:1-17—NRSV).

"No!" Paul shouts at the distortion. In Christ we are called to increase our moral sensitivity and responsibility! And his message constitutes a large order. Are we up to it? "Yes!" Is his answer, and here is his reasoning: It is his conviction that, during the process of our "conversion" from trying to do it ourselves to trusting God (the basic meaning of the word "faith" as used in the New Testament), the gift of grace *transforms* us.

In another of his letters he declares:

"Anyone who is joined to Christ is a new being: the old has gone, the new has come. All this is done by God, who through Christ, changed us from enemies into his friends and gave us the task of making others his friends also" (1 Corinthians 5:17-18—TEV).

In the NRSV the words "new being" are translated "new creation," suggesting that the process of conversion re-creates us so that we are *no longer* what we *were*. As new beings or creations, we no longer lean toward immorality for, as Paul says in his first Corinthian letter, "...we have the *mind* of Christ (1 Corinthians 2:16b—NRSV).

In short, on the issue of responsibility, Jesus' command to operate by the ethic of love is not a step *down* to *less* moral responsibility but a step *up* to *more*. In other words, love demands of us more than law!

As we think about Jesus' call to the ethic of love, transcending rules and regulations, some may wonder if that is specific enough in its direction.

For example, I sometimes hear folk say, "If you do away with the many prescriptions and prohibitions of religion, you will simply be lost." If you are one who is thinking that way, consider that, in addition to the fact that those who trust God's grace are transformed into new creations, we are also given the gift of the Holy Spirit to guide us.

You may remember on that Day of Pentecost which marks the birthday of the church, the Apostle Peter was proclaiming the Good News of God's actions in Jesus as the Christ, when some in his audience exclaimed, "What shall we do?" Because of their conviction that they were outside of God's will, they wanted instruction on how to correct that situation. Peter's response came in these words: *"Repent and be baptized every one of you in the name of Jesus Christ so that your sins may be forgiven; and you will receive the gift of the Holy Spirit. For, the promise is for you, for your children, and for all who are far away, everyone whom the Lord our God calls to him* (Acts 2:36-39).

The validity of Peter's response is affirmed throughout the New Testament. People who say "Yes" to Christ's invitation to follow in his way are given the gift of the Holy Spirit. Paul writes: "Do you know that your body is the temple of the Holy Spirit within you..." (I Corinthians 6:19—NRSV)?

Now, and here is the point regarding the guiding role of the Holy Spirit in our living through the ethic of love: living within us, the Holy Spirit becomes our Divine Guide. Jesus declares, "When the Spirit of truth comes, he will *guide* you into all truth…" John 16:13—NRSV).

Think of how astounding this is: We have our own *inner compass* that enables us to discern what is right or wrong in all situations we may face!! For me, that means I don't have to consult a book of rules and regulations. Rather, I listen to my inner being where both the mind of Christ and the Holy Spirit reside to provide guidance toward truth! My task, not always easy, is to listen, discern, and follow.

The point is this: To commit to the ethic of love, we have a greater responsibility, along with the nature, guidance, and power to assume that responsibility. That's a beautiful thing!

Now, please, let me express a concern: when I began to contemplate the profound nature of Christ's call to the ethic of love, I could hear clearly his call to love God with my whole being and my neighbor as myself. However, convinced that in these days of coming to grips with our natural environment's vulnerability to damage and destruction, I was having difficulty with what I perceived to be an absence of any reference to loving that natural world.

I was asking, out loud, on occasion, "Why, Jesus, did you leave out an instruction to love the creation of which we are a part—plants and animals like our little Yorkie, Star? My struggle with that issue became a teaching and learning moment for me. Thinking and praying about it, I began to search—re-reading the Bible, using the tools of theological reflection in search of connections, discussing the issue with colleagues, and the like. As I read again the creation stories from *Genesis*, I heard anew God's affirmation of the natural world's beauty and value. I remembered the ways in which Jesus spoke reverently about the birds of the air and the lilies of the fields; how he would often retreat into the wilderness—away from the crowds—to find peace and guidance. I even went to the book of *Revelation* to be reminded that God's intention is not to destroy the world of creation but to renew it; that there is to be a time when there will be a new heaven and a new earth and that it is precisely there that God intends to dwell. I remember those words of the Lord's Prayer, "...Thy kingdom come, Thy will be done on *earth* as it is in *heaven*...."

Deeper reflection resulted in more confidence that my concern for loving the natural world was legitimate. Why, then, did Jesus not mention it in the Great Command to love God and neighbor? Backed into the corner by that dilemma, it occurred to me that I may have an inadequate perception of who God is whom Jesus tells us to love with our whole being.

Many years ago, I abandoned the thought of God as an entity or object. Such thinking was just not reasonable. Besides it dwarfs God's nature and majesty. But in rejecting such limited imagery, had I missed the possibility that there were other limitations I had placed upon God, limitations that may be blocking my ability to detect in Jesus' Great Commandment a need to love the natural world?

In a discussion with some of my pastoral colleagues, I raised the issue. They seemed to sense my dilemma and told me about some reading they had been doing; particularly, some writing by contemporary author, Richard Rohr. They indicated that Rohr is addressing some of the issues of my concern, and suggested that I acquire his book, *The Universal Christ*. Simultaneously, conversation was circulating in our church about the beauty of Diana Butler Bass' book, *Grounded*, a book I had recently added to my personal library. On returning to my office/study at home, I immediately ordered a copy of Rohr's book. While I awaited its arrival, I read Bass' *Grounded.* In the very first chapter, titled "Dirt," she shares a quote from an author/farmer, Forrest Pritchard, whom she had met at a farmer's market where, along with his farm produce, he was selling copies of his book, *Gaining Ground*. In that book Pritchard describes a mystical experience he had experienced with the soil of his farm:

A small swath of earth was now revealed. The soil...was soft and dark. I slid my fingers into the dirt, cupping a handful of earth to my nose. The aroma of the broken ground was profoundly rich, at once mysterious and inviting; in the depth of winter—with pastures grazed low, the sycamores stark and leafless, the creek banks rimmed with ice, and the sky a gray blanket spread from mountaintop to mountaintop—here the earth abided. The soft warmth spoke to me, saying, *I am waiting now, but I will be ready. We are mutual participants, your and I, intertwined.* **1**

Reflecting on her conversation with Pritchard, Bass writes: "He did not use the word 'God' but he was talking about religion—although not institutional religion, of course. Rather he was explaining what is perhaps the source of the most primal of all human impulses toward God—the fertile land." **2**

To point up the significance of Pritchard's experience, Bass references the thinking of Sallie McFague:

Theologian Sally McFague sounds a note that harmonizes with Forrest Pritchard's experience when she writes: 'God's love is the power that moves the galaxies and that breathes in our bodies. One way to imagine this relationship between God and the world is with the metaphor of *the world as God's body*' (italics mine). **3**

Bass continues and expands with a quote from McFague's essay, *The Body of God: An Ecological Theology:*

The world, the universe, is the "body of God"; all matter, all flesh, all myriad beings, things, and processes that continue physical reality are in God and of God. God is not just spirit, but also body. Hence, God can be thought of in organic terms, as the vast interrelated network of beings that compose our universe. The "glory of God then, is not just heavenly, but earthly. **4**

McFague's metaphor for the universe, the "Body of God," may sound a little *New Age-y*. To those of you who may be acquainted with various schools of philosophy it may sound *pantheistic.* While her metaphor may sound that way, I suggest it is not. It's more in line with the classic theology of Paul Tillich, a magnificent 20th century theologian who popularized the concept that God is not appropriately perceived as an objective entity located someplace distant from earth, but, rather, is more appropriately understood—in terms of nearness—as the *ground of being* whose *being* is reflected in everything that has existence.

Some of you may remember a book from the 1960's written by Bishop John A.T. Robinson which bore the title *Honest to God.* There Robinson takes Tillich's concept of God as the "ground of being" and renders it meaningful to a generation exhausted from thinking of God as *up there* or *out there,* similar to an orbiting satellite existing, like other things in creation, as an objective entity to be found and examined.

Bass' and McFague's insights regarding the presence of God's being in all existing things were beginning to unravel my dilemma. I could feel its knotty character beginning to loosen.

In a few days Richard Rohr's, *The Universal Christ,* arrived and I dove into it like a hungry man at a banquet.

Allow me to introduce him: Rohr is a globally recognized ecumenical teacher who bears witness to the universal awakening within Christian mysticism and the Perennial Tradition. The author of numerous books, including, *A Spring Within Us* (2018), *Just This* (2018), *The Divine Dance* (2016) and *Breathing Under Water* (2016), Rohr is a Franciscan priest of the New Mexico Province and founder of the Center for Action and Contemplation in Albuquerque, New Mexico, where he also serves as Academic Dean of the Living School for Action and Contemplation.

He is a strong proponent of what he calls an *incarnational worldview* which he describes as:

"...the profound recognition of the presence of the divine in literally 'every *thing*' and 'every *one*.' It is the key to mental and spiritual health, as well as to a kind of basic contentment and happiness. An incarnational worldview is the only way we can reconcile our inner worlds with the outer one, unity with diversity, physical with spiritual, individual with corporate, and divine with human....The full Christian leap of faith is trusting that Jesus *together with Christ gave us one human but fully accurate window into the Eternal Now that we call God* (John 8:58, Colossians 1:15, Hebrews 1:3, 2 Peter 3:8). This is a leap of faith that many believe they have made when they say 'Jesus is God.' But, strictly speaking, those words are not theologically correct.

Christ is God and Jesus is the Christ's historical manifestation in time.

Jesus is a Third Someone, not just God and not just man, but God and human together.

Such is the unique and central message of Christianity and it has massive theological, psychological, and political implications— and very good ones at that. But if we cannot put these two seeming opposites of God and human together in Jesus Christ, we usually cannot put these together in ourselves, or in the rest of the physical universe. This has been our major impasse up to now. Jesus was supposed to be the code breaker, but without uniting him to Christ, we lost the core of what Christianity might have become.

A merely personal God becomes tribal and sentimental, and a merely universal God never leaves the realm of abstract theory and philosophical principles. But when we learn to put them together, Jesus and Christ give us a God who is both *personal* and *universal.* **5**

You may need to take a moment to let all that sink in. I assure you it is worth both your and my reflection.

"Incarnational worldview" is one of Rohr's terms throughout the book. Another is "The Christ Mystery," which is what the previous quote is talking about. Hear him as he continues to elaborate:

"The Christ Mystery anoints all physical matter with eternal purpose from the very beginning....

Ironically, millions of the very devout who are waiting for the "Second Coming" have largely missed the first—and the third! I'll say it again, God loves things by becoming them. And...God did so in the creation of the universe and of Jesus, and continues to do so in the ongoing human Body of Christ (1 Corinthians 12:12ff.) and even in simple elements of bread and wine....

For me, a true comprehension of the full Christ Mystery is the key to the foundational reform of the Christian religion, which alone will move us beyond any attempts to corral or capture God into our exclusive group. As the New Testament dramatically and clearly puts it, "Before the world was made, we have been chosen in Christ...claimed as God's own, and chosen from the very beginning" (Ephesians 1:3, 11) "so that he could bring everything together under the headship of Christ" (1:10). *If all this is true; we have a theological basis for a very natural religion that includes everybody. The problem is solved from the beginning. Take your Christian head off, shake it wildly, and put it back on!"* **6**

One of Rohr's points is that God's creating the world constitutes a very important *first* incarnation which would be followed much later by the life and ministry of Jesus in whom God was incarnate.

As the *Genesis* account makes clear, as God completes each phase of creation, there is a pause and God reflects upon the fact that each of those is *good*. An element in the goodness is the fact that God is joined to creation in such a way that God is reflected in every *thing* and every *one*, and that God, from the very beginning, chose and blessed it.

The Psalmist captures the integral connection between creation and God beautifully as he describes the natural world's loving response to its Maker:

Praise the Lord! Praise the Lord from the heavens; praise him, all his angels; praise him all his host!

Praise him, sun and moon, praise him, all you shining stars! Praise him, you highest heavens, and you waters above the heavens!

Let them praise the name of the Lord for he commanded and they were created. He established them forever and ever; he fixed their bounds which cannot be passed.

Praise the Lord from the earth, you sea monsters and all deeps, fire and hail, snow and frost, stormy wind fulfilling his command!

Mountains and all hills, fruit trees and all cedars! Wild animals and all cattle, creeping things and flying birds!

Kings of the earth and all peoples, princes and all rulers of the earth! Young men and women alike, old and young together!

Let them praise the name of the Lord, for his name alone is

exalted; his glory is above earth and heaven. He has raised up a horn for his people, praise for all his faithful, for the people of Israel who are close to him.

Praise the Lord (Psalm 148—NRSV)!

Rohr asks his readers to consider the calculation showing that between the Big Bang and the onset of events in the Bible, beginning with the call of Abraham to be the father of what would become Israel, is a period of *13.7 billion years* (Italics mine). In light of that, I ask you, is it reasonable to assume that during that span of time, God was establishing *no* relationship with creation, that God was *not* addressing the world of creation until the call of Abraham and the birth of Jesus in the last nanosecond of geological time? To my mind that is not a reasonable assumption. So, I find meaning in Rohr's notion that from the beginning, God had identified so deeply with creation—embedding with it—that all of nature was enjoying a relationship with God, being sustained in its "goodness," by God's Spirit within it; that from its beginning and through all phases of its development creation, including humanity, had in its heart a thirst and hunger for God that was being met in a dynamic relationship with God.

It is this recognition and realization of God embedded in the natural world that finally has enabled me to acknowledge that creation is an integral part of God.

Now when I hear Jesus calling us to love God with our whole being, I realize that such a love includes loving the natural world, the "Body of God," to use McFague's metaphoric description.

This transition in my thinking, aided by the creative theological reflections of Bass, McFague and Rohr, has awakened within me both latent and new dimensions of understanding. This awakening has deepened my comprehension of God's nature: God is not an entity, object, or thing circumscribed by the limitations thereof! God is the *ground of being,* in every *thing* and every *one*. God is more than *a* god, *a* being, *an* entity. God is in all things and all persons. God's presence in the natural world cannot be ignored.

Loving God with one's whole being is both challenged and empowered by such an understanding. It challenges us to move beyond our tendency to diminish God. Such love invites us to see God everywhere reflected in the natural world. It challenges our traditional tribalism which perceives God as limited to one distinctive, place, way, race, religion, nation, world, etc.

It is my experience this recognition has brought *freedom;* particularly a freedom for openness to and for acceptance of those who are different from me and mine. (In Chapter 3, I will describe this freedom in more detail).

Some years ago, when scholar J.B. Phillips asked

the world, *Is Your God Too Small*?, he was onto something that is staggeringly significant: to reflect upon whether, indeed, we attempt to dwarf God and, thereby, fail to be caught up in the awe of the magnitude and inclusiveness of the One who brings everything into existence and who is reflected in its face, whatever species that face represents!

This broader thinking about God's nature not only provides freedom for *openness*, I find it to be *empowering* as well. Its very broadness is both inspirational and motivational. In other words, the bigness of God is in itself an empowering force. Because that bigness is pure love whose energy becomes a powerful magnet capable of drawing everything and everyone into its embrace, literally saving them from destruction.

Surely Jesus had this in mind when he declared, "And I, when I am lifted up from the earth, will draw all people to myself" (John 12:32—NRSV). And no wonder St. Augustine, moved by the deep inspiration of experience, so eloquently prayed to God, "Our hearts are restless, until they find their rest in Thee" (Augustine of Hippo, *Confessions*).

Finally, my dilemma is solved! When Jesus commands me to love God with my whole being, I am now aware that includes all creation. My dilemma, spawned by an inadequate perception of God, is solved in an experience of the awesome scope of God's being.

From his instruction about loving *God* with our whole being, Jesus now moves to direct us toward loving our *neighbor*.

At the outset, I was thinking in terms of the "two-ness" of these commands. In fact, in the scripture reference (Matthew 11:34-40), after declaring the direction for us to love God with our whole being, Jesus continues, "And a *second* is like it: "You shall love your neighbor as yourself." You see, then, they do constitute two distinctive commands. But the distance from loving God to loving one's neighbor is not great. I have made the case that loving God includes the breadth of the natural world which is so integrally related to God. That natural world includes, of course, us humans. In that sense, therefore, the distance is closed. But practically speaking—and Jesus seems always to be practical—he focuses specifically upon our obligation toward one another as human beings.

Another way of viewing the issue is to view human beings as having a problem with relationships (disharmonious, fractured, and troubled) which appears more serious and complex than that in the remainder of nature. This seems to be the case particularly among humans who, like the Pharisees see themselves as better than others in such a way that they proceed to draw lines of distinction and exclusion between themselves and others. Perhaps that's why Jesus seems at home with the separation of our responsibility to love God from that of loving our neighbor into two. Yet, there is a sense in which we must not allow ourselves to separate God and neighbor too radically, as though they are distinctive, watertight compartments, lest we begin to think we can respond to one without the other. The two are joined at the hip *and* at the heart. Consider, for example, John's comment on that connection:

"Those who say, 'I love God,' and hate their brothers or sisters, are liars; for those who do not love a brother or sister whom they have seen, cannot love God whom they have not seen. The commandment we have from him is this: those who love God must love their brothers and sisters also! (I John 4:20-12—NRSV)

This emphasis upon the connection between loving God and neighbor seems relevant in every generation. Ours is no exception, for I hear and read of numerous persons who consider themselves to be followers of Christ, who have developed a puzzling expertise in despising, even rejecting, designated other folk. For example, Facebook seems constantly to carry posts by folk who see themselves as robust Christians; yet have designated Muslims as targets for exclusion and derision. One such recent post suggested that we make clear that Jesus is the only way to God precisely *because* of its power to offend Muslims. It encouraged readers to "flood Facebook" with such posts for the expressed purpose of intimidating Muslims.

In my years of pastoral service, I have known church folk who gave verbal affirmation to their love for God, while simultaneously rejecting a fellow human being who had offended them or who did not measure up to their expectation.

Jesus taught the necessity of loving others, even those who are offensive to us:

"You have heard that it was said, 'You shall love your neighbor and hate your enemy. But I say unto you, love your enemies and pray for those who persecute you, so that you may be children of your Father in heaven, for he makes his sun to rise on the evil and on the good, and send rain on the righteous and on the unrighteous. For if you love those who love you, what reward do you have? Do not even the tax collectors do the same? And if you greet only your brothers and sisters, what more are you doing than others? Do not even the Gentiles do the same? (Matthew 5:43-47—NRSV).

During my college years I became acquainted with a pastor who seemed to have heard and taken Jesus' message to heart. He was a frequent speaker at our chapel services. Constantly, he pleaded with us to proclaim the gospel in love and, always, to avoid using the Bible as a club with which to maul folk.

As I am writing, there comes to mind an experience in my civic club. We had a great group of guys and a very rich fellowship at our gatherings. Many life-long friendships grew out of that experience for me and for others.

In the mid 1980's we became sensitized to the fact that our club membership was exclusively male. This was called to our attention when our membership committee announced to the Board that a female had petitioned us for membership. Vigorous discussion ensued in which pro and con positions were taken on the issue. One person who had a tendency to be boisterous, obnoxious and offensive about many issues got on his high horse about how accepting women was not an option for us. "We are exclusively a male club," he shouted. "We don't need any damn women in here! Can you imagine having in our membership someone who bleeds every twenty- eight days?!" That was a real turnoff for me.

When I arrived home in the evening, I described to my wife that experience at the club. Already aware of my discomfort with the individual, she was shocked when I exclaimed, "This guy is stupid and uncouth! I have decided not to speak to or associate with him ever again. I will just ignore such ignorance."

I was bothered all week with the experience when I began to realize that what bothered me most was my reaction to my offensive club brother. My conscience was stinging both my mind and my body. I prayed for a week for God's guidance on the matter when one day I awoke with clarity. The position I had taken was not tenable! How could I be a follower of Jesus and draw such an exclusionary line between myself and another human being? I knew I had to abandon my determination not to relate to this fellow.

At the next meeting I intentionally greeted him and inquired about his health. "How are you? I asked. He responded, "Not doing too well, Jim, I've developed some health problems."

Weeks went by and an announcement was made that he had been taken to the hospital, having lost consciousness at home. All day I struggled with whether to visit him there. The next day I was sitting at his bedside. He seemed very glad to see me. Our conversation was relaxed and easy. At one point he looked into my eyes and said, "Jim, I have admired the times when you have addressed our club on special occasions like Christmas. I've listened to your remarks as our Board meetings. I want you to know that I respect you and where you're coming from." Then tears welled up in his eyes as he continued, "I may not make it through this experience. If I don't, would you consider doing my memorial service?" A feeling of warmth came over me. Suddenly, barriers that I had erected between us were rapidly melting under the warm rays generated by the union of our two hearts. I responded with something like, "Well, of course, if something happens to you before it happens to me, I'll be honored to lead your service."

On subsequent visits to the hospital I could see that his condition was improving. Soon he had returned home and, not long thereafter, was back in our club meetings.

I noticed that his boisterous spirit, with its delight in stirring the anger of peers, had given way to a more compassionate and considerate demeanor. It was as though he had begun to care what others thought. I noticed, too, that he would seek me out at the meetings for conversation. When Christmas Eve rolled around, I looked out into the congregation and there he sat—right on the front row with a smile as wide as the Mississippi!

He became a friend. This person who was on record as not caring much for religion or for religious persons, was developing into a person of reverence and respect. He is gone now. Frequently—as now in this writing—I see Jesus' wisdom in encouraging all his followers to move beyond our tendency to cut off the offender and to designate others as enemies to be ignored, if not excluded. I am pleased that God granted me the grace to re-approach the relationship with my club brother, resulting in transforming an ugly disposition into genuine friendship. I've concluded that when I get to heaven, one of the persons I will see there—by the grace and mercy and transforming power of God—is my Kiwanis friend, sitting with the saints and, maybe, even singing in the Choir!

In his reminder that we are to love others, Jesus sets a high standard by which to measure the love we are to have for them. "Love your neighbor as *yourself*."

Jesus seems to assume that each of us has an innate sense of self-love, at least self-concern without which we would be in a heap of trouble, refusing—or unable—to take the precautions necessary to protect ourselves from the danger or to execute plans enabling us to meet the needs of ourselves and our families. We are to love others that much. What we do to enrich and enhance the well-being of ourselves, we are willing to do for others. And it is a matter of *doing* or *acting*. The word Jesus uses for "love" is a form of the Greek, *agape*, which is given more to action than to feeling. It may be easier to say to another, "I love you," that is, I have a very warm feeling for you, than to act on behalf of the other. It's love in action that counts.

For example, in his first of three letters, John echoes the teaching of Jesus when he writes, "Little children, let us love not in word or speech, but in truth and action" (I John 3:18—NRSV).

On another occasion, following Jesus' affirmation of his verbal commitment to loving his neighbor, a Pharisee asked Jesus, "Who is my neighbor" (Luke 10:29—NRSV)? Jesus responds with the Parable of the Good Samaritan to make the point that loving our neighbor is expressed in compassionate action toward her or him; particularly when that neighbor is in need and especially when the neighbor belongs to a group that is popularly rejected. Jesus, therefore, is reaffirming his conviction that love for another is expressed in clear action on her or his behalf, i.e., we do for others what we would do or have done for ourselves.

In his response to the Pharisaic lawyer, Jesus is reminding him and all of us of the essence of authentic religion: it always expresses love toward God and others. Doing this, it rises above any tendency we have not to recognize, affirm and reverence the Creator and Sustainer of all life, God. Creation, including humanity, is at its best when it lovingly affirms this Source of all things and moves on to the point of loving all that the Source loves; loving all both in word and in deed. Because all created things have their being in God, *the ground of being,* each of us is at our best when we recognize and affirm the sacred dignity within every *thing* and ever *one*, expressing admiration, acceptance and love for them. In other words, to live authentically is to love! Jesus now brings his conversation with the lawyer to an end with this: "On these two commandments hang all the law and the prophets" (22:40—NRSV). What does he mean? Having repeated the commands to love God and to love our neighbor, Jesus seems to be suggesting that such love is the key to understanding and doing the will of God. To my mind, he is saying that being faithful is not primarily about following rules and regulations but about loving action in all our relationships.

Interestingly, *The Living Bible* offers this paraphrase of the passage:

"All other commandments and all the demands of the prophets stem from these two laws and are fulfilled if you obey them. Keep only these and you will find that you are obeying all the others."

Through the years I have often been asked, "Pastor, how can I be sure that I am living within the will of God?" or, "How can I know I am saved?"

I sensed the insecurity behind the question. I also sensed the need to be "certain" about the relationship. That need for certainty made me a little antsy. Ultimately, faith (trust) defies the limitations of rationality or the need for a feeling of certitude. Yet the question is a fair one and I have always tried to take it seriously.

My usual response has been to invite the inquirer to consider and to trust this passage from Matthew about the centrality of love as a sign of an authentic relationship with God. The approach has often been well received as inquirers have recognized the importance of loving and of recognizing that love as a sign of an authentic relationship with God and with others.

Here is the crux of the matter:

"Beloved, let us love one another, because love is from God; everyone who loves is born of God and knows God...God is love, and those who abide in love abide in God, and God abides in them. Love has been perfected among us in this: that we may have boldness on the day of judgment because as he is, so are we in this world. There is no fear in love, but perfect love casts out fear...We love because he first loved us (I John 4:7, 16-19--NRSV).

Love is the way of Christ. Christ calls us to walk in love and assures us that our love for one another is the strongest indicator that we are together in him.

No wonder, then, that Jesus follows with an indication that on these two commandments—loving God and one another—hang all the Law and the prophets. I take this to mean that being at one with God and everything around us has more to do with the loving lifestyle than with what, intellectually, we believe about this or that.

Someone has said, "Jesus Christ is not about religion, it's about relationships." That statement is becoming more profound to my mind as the days go by.

In this chapter I have explored Jesus' Great Commandment in some detail and have declared that living by the ethic of loving God and others is the essence of Christian discipleship. To my mind and spirit, that represents a huge transition in my thinking about the nature of religion and in determining the posture of my behavior before God and God's creation. It will not surprise the reader when I indicate that there are multiple implications of such a position. In the upcoming chapter, I invite you to consider some of those.

CHAPTER 3

Some Implications of the Loving Lifestyle

"Only a free soul will never grow old" —Jean Paul Richter

The first of these implications focuses upon the gift of freedom itself, freedom from so many of the restrictions that institutional religion places upon us both in terms of thought and action. The remaining implications are derived from the first—the gift of freedom—and focus upon aspects of freedom that emerge from that basic gift.

We Are Given Freedom

I believe every person yearns to be free. Particularly in the tradition of democracy, freedom is held to be of precious value. Some of the greatest struggles of humanity have been either the struggle to become free or the struggle to maintain our freedom.

We frequently speak of our freedom to express our convictions in public places, the freedom to worship according to the dictates of our own hearts, the freedom to own property, to vote and to be considered equal with others. In the United

States—as in much of the western world—these are recognized and affirmed in our basic governing documents.

Few such freedoms existed at the time of Jesus' earthly ministry; yet Jesus experienced a deep sense of freedom and led his followers to experience it as well. As the movement expanded, breaking out of the boundaries of Judaism and penetrating the Gentile world, Paul, the Apostle, held that Christ had brought us to experience a freedom that he felt was foundational; one that lay deeper than the social and political ones. As with Jesus, Paul felt that both the cause and the reflection of this freedom were manifested in our love for God and for one another. Freedom's *foundational* character is reflected in the way in which it affects our relationship to two major forces that tend to imprison us, namely, our *human nature* and *religion* itself.

Our *human nature* is vulnerable to becoming its own slave as it allows itself to be so preoccupied with its own personal security that it becomes relatively insensitive both to God and to others.

Here is how it works. Self-preoccupation occurs when our sense of well-being is threatened. For example, when our feelings of insecurity press us to ask: Will I have a place to live and enough to eat? Will I be able to earn enough money to rise to a nice level of comfort? Will I find acceptance among my peers and will I be as popular as others?

As these questions suggest, others begin to be perceived as competitors and, sometimes as adversaries. We compete with them to acquire our basic needs and many of our desires. The competition is not always friendly. It can become adversarial.

As a result, anxiety rears its head in our hearts, anxiety about our own security: Will I get there before someone else does? Will there be anything left? The higher the level of anxiety, the more we become preoccupied with our own sense of security, so we begin to be obsessed to the point of either becoming insensitive to others or antagonistic toward them.

Our focus becomes our project to establish our own security. The value of those around us, even the value of God gets diminished or lost. As this occurs, we find ourselves in deep trouble. Our lives become a heavy burden. The sense of adventure and fulfillment are severely impacted.

What happens when we live by the ethic of love for God and others is liberation from such an existential jailhouse. The dynamics of love seize any sign of preoccupation with our self-security and compel us to refocus upon God and others, but in such a way that the self is not destroyed, for, as Jesus points out in the second of the two great commandments—we are to love our neighbors *as we love ourselves*. It's a process of projecting beyond ourselves, there to establish trusting and compassionate relationships that deliver a life-giving balance to the equation of living.

Living by the ethic of loving God and loving one another is profoundly about freedom—freedom from inappropriate and paralyzing preoccupation with the self.

So, one of humanity's binding forces, is that part of our human nature that gravitates toward self-obsession. This has been the case throughout human history.

Another of those binding forces, I believe, has been—and in important ways—continues to be religion, the type of religion that tends to rob us of freedom.

In this context I feel it is important to emphasize that the root meaning and character of religion is not negative. For example, consider that the Latin root for "religion" is *religio* which means faith, trust, love, devotion, an attitude toward the divine or nature. But, as it is perceived by many of our contemporaries, that positive dimension of religion has been seriously eroded or has completely changed.

In his 1963 book, *The Meaning and End of Religion*, Wilfred Cantwell Smith, a professor of comparative religion at Harvard, pointed out that the end of religion had come. Did he mean something negative with his observation? No. He did not see the end of religion as unfortunate for, in his view "religion" had taken a turn which had changed its original positive meaning into something negative. He proceeds to point out that the newer definition, which began to emerge as early as the seventeenth century, had begun to conceptualize religion as a system of ideas or beliefs about God. He writes:

In pamphlet after pamphlet, treatise after treatise, decade after decade, the notion was driven home that religion is something that one believes or does not believe, something whose propositions are true or are not true, something whose *locus* is the realm of the intelligible, is up for inspection before the speculative mind." **1**

It was this "intellectualization" of religion into a belief system that Smith saw coming to an end.

Diana Butler Bass confirms Smith's conclusion regarding this unfortunate change of meaning. In her book, *Christianity After Religion,* she writes:

"In modern times, religion became indistinguishable from systematizing ideas about God, religious institutions, and human beings; it categorized, organized, objectified, and divided people into exclusive worlds of right versus wrong, true versus false, 'us' verses 'them.'" **2**

In short, earlier, *religio* referred to "something in men's *hearts*" (Smith). However, in modern times, *religion* has morphed into something in men's *minds,* having to do more with doctrines to be believed than a behavior-modifying attitude toward God and all of life.

I suggest that along with this transition from heart to mind came also a *casuistic* mentality, i.e., the thought of living in response to a set of expectations and rules—an "ought" mentality as in "These things I *ought* or *have* to do in order to gain acceptance or approval." That path developed into a legalistic system of expectations of dos and don'ts, much like the Pharisaical legalism which Jesus encountered in the first century. Thus, as Pharisaical religion had become burdensome (see Matthew 23:4), religion, in its *modern* sense, had morphed into a similar burdensome system.

Whether in that first century setting or in our own, I hold that the Great Commandment constitutes a divine invitation to leave our preoccupation with rules, regulations, and right beliefs, and return to our hearts where love for God and others sets us free.

Ecumenism (the spirit of cooperation among religious denominations) has improved the religious scene considerably. For example, these days, Lutherans, Presbyterians, Methodists, and others can fellowship comfortably with one another. Yet there continue to be deep doctrinal divisions within the institutional church, so deep that, in some cases,

Christians of one denomination are not approved to participate in the Lord's Supper or Holy Communion with Christians of another. I suggest that such prevalence of discrimination reflects the Church's continuing captivity to doctrinal rationalism.

The polls of which I am aware show all the major denominations, even the Southern Baptists, loosing membership and experiencing dramatic decline in worship attendance. I believe that a part of the reason for this loss lies in the fact that a significant number, both within the institution and outside, no longer see many of the beliefs and practices of organized religion as either relevant or reasonable.

Consider the following:

In the United States, somewhere in the range of 25 to 30 percent of the population under thirty neither attend religious services nor have any religious preference, although about half of the unaffiliated group still say that they believe in God or understand themselves to be spiritual. Whatever else may be said of them, they are profoundly disappointed in religion, religious ideologies, and organizations as those currently exist. In a 2004 survey, the Barna organization found that young adults who are outside of church hold intensely negative views of Christianity: 91 percent think that Christianity is "anti-homosexual." 87 percent say Christians are "judgmental,' 85 percent accuse churchgoers of being "hypocritical," and 72 percent say Christianity is "out of touch with reality." Only 41 percent think that Christianity seems "genuine or real" or "makes sense," while 30 percent think that it is "relevant to your life." **3**

This survey suggests to me that religion is perceived by many moderns as that which attempts to put people into straightjackets that leave little room for freedom of spiritual movement. As a result, it seems out of touch with real experience and emphasizes that which seems not to be of major significance to modern thinking and the perception of modern needs for fulfillment.

This information represents both something negative and positive. The above survey is shared in Diana Butler Bass' book, *Christianity After Religion.* Her context for including it is one in which she is making the case that we may be facing the end of church but the birth of a new spiritual awakening. Part of her reasoning for this conviction is that religious institutions are no longer perceived as meeting the needs of deep spiritual yearning that exists in the hearts of modern folk; not a yearning for "religion," but a yearning for "spiritual fulfillment."

The point being made here is that this *type* of religion (as a belief system) is coming to an end. In face of that, I am suggesting that the love ethic of the Great Commandment offers an alternative which leads to more authentic, relevant, and effective living, freeing us from the kind of religion that stifles those essential elements that constitute spiritual fulfillment.

It is not surprising, therefore, that the Apostle Paul gives this dramatic exhortation in his *Letter to the Galatians*: "For freedom Christ has set us free. Stand firm, therefore, and do not submit again to a yoke of slavery" (5:1--NRSV).

Freedom for Experiential Faith

Numerous scholars have made the case that the meaning of the word "faith" has undergone a change similar to that of religion. For example, if you are at a social gathering and someone ventures to ask "What is your faith?" Most likely the inquirer is interested in learning about your religious label. I grew up in a religious environment in which others were interested in one's belief about doctrine: Do you believe Jesus is divine? What is your view of the Bible? Or do you consider the Bible to be the divinely inspired Word of God? What's your view of baptism? etc. That environment continues to be with us.

I am endeavoring to make the case that this *transition* in our understanding of "faith" represents an erosion of its meaning. It is not my intention to declare doctrine as unimportant, for, in my opinion, the formulation of doctrine represents an effort to render matters of faith more *understandable* (though, sometimes, it does not). However, I do feel that belief in doctrine or other creedal formulations may stand in the way of a richer experience with God. For example, I sense that some are satisfied if they think that they believe the right things which seems to arrest their progress toward forming a life-giving relationship with God and with God's creation. Thus, belief systems sometimes end up as a substitute for spiritual experience.

As early as 1955 noted Jewish scholar, Abraham Joshua Heschel, wrote:

" When faith is completely replaced by creed, worship by discipline, love by habit; when the crisis of today is ignored because of the splendor of the past; when faith becomes an heirloom rather than a living fountain; when religion speaks only in the name of authority rather than with the voice of compassion…the message becomes meaningless." 4

It is my desire, here, to point out that giving priority to the Great Commandment's direction toward loving God and our neighbor has helped many to move beyond the limiting, even stultifying, influence of religious dogmatism, legalism, moralism, and the like, that which I am calling a rule book mentality.

An example in my personal journey is my long felt need to do solid theological reflection on the nature of God. Whereas, earlier I thought of God as an entity "up there" or "out there" which produced the element of distance (as well as *cognitive dissonance*, given my modern understanding of the cosmos) I have come to experience God in much nearer terms as "the ground of being" (Tillich).

That journey has been set in motion and sustained by the powerful vision of the Great Commandment's exhortation to love God with my entire being. That vision has inspired me to open my mind, heart and soul to the One who surrounds and dwells within me, an experience that continues to draw me into a personal relationship with God's wonder. This has resulted in an experience of God moving closer to me and me moving closer to God in a mutual embrace between Creator and creature.

Thomas Merton wrote about the effective role of contemplation in making more intimate our relationship with the Divine. Contemplation relies less upon the role of intellectual formulations and doctrinal/creedal formulations (which appeal to the intellect) and more on spiritual union which appeals to the experiential side of our nature.

In 1964, with a group of fellow seminarians I had the privilege of visiting the monastery where Merton was a monk. We spent a good hour dialoguing with him around the issue of contemplative prayer. Following that encounter I acquired several of his books on the subject. As a result of my exposure to this wonderful man of God, and the application of some of his insights, I found my experience with God to be deepening.

In my earlier book, *Mining for Meaning* (2013), I described this experience in greater detail, sharing some specific illustrations of its effects. For example, there, I describe a mode of experiential trust, enabled by contemplation, that moves one beyond an ordinary state of consciousness into what Stanislav Grof's transpersonal psychology calls a "holotropic" mode. In that mode one becomes more open to life's realities, whether in reference to mundane things like rivers and animals or the

Divine itself. While Grof, not a theologian but a psychologist, does not reference Divinity as such, I have utilized his perspective and methodology as a tool to enrich my fellowship with God.

In the following quotation, Grof describes the scope of what he calls the "holotropic" (beyond the ordinary) mode of consciousness:

> Experienced extension of consciousness in the holotropic mode is not limited to the world of biology: it can include macroscopic and microscopic phenomena of inorganic nature. Subjects have repeatedly reported that they had experientially identified with the water in rivers and oceans. The various forms of fire, with the earth and mountains, or with forces unleashed in natural catastrophes, such as electric storms, earthquakes, tornadoes, and volcanic eruptions. Equally common is identification with specific materials—diamond, and other precious stones, quartz, crystal, amber, granite, iron, steel, quicksilver, or gold. These experiences can extend into the micro world and involve the dynamic structure of molecules and atoms...even electromagnetic forces and subatomic particles.... It seems that every process in the universe that one can observe objectively in the ordinary state of consciousness also has a subjective experiential counterpart in the holotropic mode" 5.

Reflecting upon Grof's findings makes it apparent that, in order to move to a consideration of consciousness that is beyond the ordinary, one must stretch beyond the comfort zone of traditional thinking and experience. I can tell you that as I have moved beyond the limited horizons of preoccupation with traditional doctrines, etc., making room for the expanded consciousness, I have experienced fresh dimensions of encountering God who seems always, to defy the limitations of

Tradition while, at the same time, coming to us in authentic ways through Tradition.

There was a time when I was reluctant to think or try new things for fear that I would break the rules of my belief system. That fear has diminished. But I am aware that to launch in that direction is to take risks. For example, we may become concerned about what others might think of us if we break out of the doctrinal system in which we have lived much of our lives to move into areas that those systems never seemed capable of anticipating. The concern is justified, for there are those who will hold one in suspicion or, indeed, reject one when she or he leaves the "herd thinking" that characterizes rulebook mentality. Moreover, when one moves toward such newness, a temporary sense of insecurity (Am I going to be lost in the shuffle?!) may result as the security blanket is taken away to be replaced by a deeper sense of security than that which has been previously known. In my own experience, being led by the ethic of loving God with my entire being provides a profound—perhaps even unimaginable—sense of security. In short, I find that when I have pulled up the anchor of my ship from its traditional mooring and opened my sails to the fresh winds of God's Holy Spirit, my ship sails directly into the *abundant life* of which Jesus spoke.

Freed from the rule book mentality by the enabling power of the Great Commandment's love ethic has not only opened a deeper experience of *God*, it has also deepened my experience of loving my *neighbor*.

I remember a time in my personal history when I chose to relate to people who shared my value system while tending to hold myself at a distance from those who did not. I was reared in a culture that clearly taught its people to gravitate toward those who were like oneself. I remember, too, how as a young man, I would resist creating relationships with girls who were of a different religious denomination than my own. If they were Methodists, they were different from me. If they were Roman Catholic, they must be from another planet! Back then, we knew there were non-Christian religions—Hindus, Muslims, Buddhists, etc. but they lived way over there across the ocean and we had few expectations of ever encountering them.

There were even certain family clans we were taught to avoid. I remember when I announced to my parents the name of my first girlfriend, Shirley____, they reacted, "No, son, surely not a ____ (her last name associated her with a family clan that grown unpopular in the community)!

That cultural context worked directly into my corresponding religious mentality of legalism. I felt pride both in those I had accepted into my circle of friends and those I had excluded from that circle.

But I kept bumping up against Jesus' refusal to draw such lines of exclusion. Early on, I had perceived Jesus' talk about loving one's neighbor as referencing those people who were deemed neighborly because they shared similar values-those who looked like and thought like me. Eventually, however, I began to realize, particularly from the Parable of the Good Samaritan, that a neighbor is a designation for all human beings we encounter. The point that the Samaritan who gave aid to the victim was from an ethnic group which had become arch enemies of the Jews, and that the victim was a Jew got my attention, sensitizing me to the *radical* nature of Jesus' love ethic. Eventually I came to realize that to live by the Great Commandment was to erase all lines by which we mentally, socially, or religiously, exclude others.

The more diverse our world becomes, the wiser I consider the Great Commandment to be. While, for many, the greater the diversity surrounding us, the more rigid our exclusion of those who are different, for those who take Jesus' teaching seriously, such exclusion is not a moral or practical option.

Jesus saw humanity—indeed creation—as a whole. Judaism of which he was an integral part came to recognize that there is a *common* humanity; that, as Luke puts in *Acts* 17:26--NRSV: "From one ancestor (other ancient manuscripts read *"From one blood)* he (God) made all nations to inhabit the whole earth...."

While there was a time in the development of Israel in which the Hebrews emphasized their distinction from other peoples, by the time of Jesus, Judaism, recognizing the value of others, devised ways for Gentiles (non-Jews) to come into their religion, albeit through ceremonies (like circumcision) that became an issue with which the early church struggled. Peter and James felt circumcision as necessary for salvation. Paul, recognizing more clearly than they that all people belonged to God and should be welcomed by faith in Christ, won the day.

Jesus was very clear—there are to be no distinctions for bias in humanity. In God, as Paul declared in Athens, "we all live and move and have our being" (Acts 17:28---KJV).

Living in our increasingly diverse world, the acceptance of others is a genuine challenge. But, amidst such diversity, we are called to define our neighbor as all other persons and "...to love our neighbor as we love ourselves."

While such expansive love is not always easy for me, I am intentional in my effort to practice it. Increasingly freed from the traditional limitations, I am able to see others in the light of Christ's value system, i.e., as persons of value and dignity who, by virtue of their humanity, deserve my love and respect. Paul's insight into the transforming effects of conversion grows in its importance for me.

He declares that, in Christ, we no longer live for ourselves and that we no longer regard others from a human (a socio-economic) point of view (see 2 Corinthians 5:15,16--NRSV).

Freedom from the rulebook mentality enables us to relate to others for the humans they are. The ethic of love calls us to relate to Democrats, Republicans, Independents or Socialists without allowing their politics to become a blocking force, and to relate to Muslims or Hindus or Buddhists as persons who, by virtue of our common humanity, deserve our love and respect.

When we are free to relate to God and others without looking at them through the prism of a rule-book mentality, rich and life-giving results occur.

Obviously, such acceptance of others does not necessitate our adoption of their values or their religion, but it does demand that we accept the fact that God accepts them as they are, just as God accepts us as we are.

Freedom to live by the ethic of love enables one to believe humbly, that there is more than one way to live authentically; that there is more than one door into the gigantic room we call love and acceptance. In my view this freedom to love God and others is much needed in a world that has become divided and exclusionary.

James Bailiff
Freedom to Become Reconcilers

As I previously acknowledged, *tribalism*—our human tendency to think and act in terms of what is best for us and ours—continues to fragment society and to pit those fragments against one another—my clan against your clan, my race against your race, my politics against your politics, my nation against your nation, etc.

Reconciliation is a process by which we are empowered to move beyond such boundaries, reaching out to embrace others, a process that continues to expand in such a way that the growth of the reconcilers exceeds that of the tribalists while, at the same time, having a compassion for the tribalists that reaches out to invite them to become a part of the community of the reconciled.

One of the issues I have encountered in my ministry of reconciliation is that of very difficult, even despicable people, those persons whose demeanor and behavior give me pause to question whether they are worthy of my efforts.

One of my friends refers to these as "extra grace required" persons. When asked for expanded comment on the meaning of that moniker, he responded, "I could refer to these folks as those stupid folks whose character is so out of sorts that they could probably never become reconciled or reconcilers. But that would reveal a shortcoming on my part at recognizing the remarkable ability of God's amazing grace both to attract and to transform. It would also reflect a tribal tendency to exclude certain types of people, something that God seems never willing to do."

Throughout my ministry—especially since learning from my friend's use of "extra grace required" to refer to those difficult people—I have attempted not to write anyone off as being ineligible for the Kingdom of God. I have found that concentrating upon bringing "extra grace" expectations into my relationship with such folk enables me more effectively to work with them. Just now, I am thinking of an individual who was very difficult to work with. In name he was a member of the reconciled community, but he was anything but a reconciler. The point in time at which I became pastor of the congregation of which he was a part, I was made aware that he was such a person.

A case in point was the process in which the congregation was considering the eradication of a policy prohibiting women from becoming Elders (a lay-oriented spiritual care position). Up to this point, the person in question had worked feverishly to torpedo the change process. At the first Elders' meeting I attended as the congregation's new pastor, the issue was on the agenda. When it was placed on the floor, immediately this fellow rose with Bible in hand, waving it and declaring, "The Word of God forbids women from entering the eldership. It clearly says that only men are eligible for that office!" The effect of his behavior was electrifying for me.

Following a time of silence, another Elder rose. With calmness, sprinkled with conviction, he offered an alternative view: "With due respect for my brother who has just spoken, there are parts of the Bible that may very well imply women ineligible for the office of Elder. However, there are other parts that emphasize the church as a new kind of community, distinctive from society's tendency to establish barriers. For example, that section in *Galatians* in which Paul writes that 'in Christ there is no longer Jew or Greek, there is no longer slave or free, there is no longer male or female; for all are one in Christ Jesus.' To me, this means that the church is called to be a community without barriers."

The process for consideration for women elders continued for a few weeks. Eventually the Elders recommended to the Board and the Congregation the gender integration of that important office. It was approved overwhelmingly.

Although there were many among us who reached out to the fellow whose dissent had been registered, he was not a happy camper and continued his attempt to control decision-making and his efforts to destroy group harmony. Some years later, when the issue of moving our congregation to a new location was considered, the individual seemed to intensify his efforts to be disruptive. I doubled down on my effort to be pastoral.

Following several months of study, a task force we called "The Committee on the Future" had found that continuing in our current location was not feasible. We were locked into very limited downtown land space and the price of purchasing contiguous property for our expansion was considered not to be economically feasible. The recommendation was made to seek a new location east of Interstate 75. It was passed by our Board and placed on the agenda of a special congregational meeting for approval.

During the few weeks between the Board's action and the time of the congregational meeting, the individual in question was actively campaigning against relocation, and announcing his intention to leave if the congregation approved the recommendation to move. Most of his criticism was focused not upon the merits and demerits of the move but upon what he perceived to be ulterior motives of our church leaders—both lay and clergy.

I felt led to visit in the individual's home to provide an ear for listening to his concerns. When I called to make the appointment, his wife was cordial and seemed happy for the suggested visit. Later, when I arrived at their home, she greeted me pleasantly, indicating that he was waiting for me in another room. I went there to meet him. He rose, shook my hand, and indicated his pleasure in my coming. He invited me to sit for conversation.

Following some pleasantries, I remarked, "I understand you are having considerable difficulty with our Board's recommendation to move our location." Immediately he responded, "I am surely against it! This is not of God and you could stop it if you wanted to!"

Thinking for a moment, I saw two parts of his statement to which I felt a response was appropriate. "You say that this decision is not of God. That interests me, could you say more." He did; much more! Subsequently, I reviewed the process out of which the decision had grown—the two-year period of study by the Committee on the Future, the Board's process of consideration leading to their recommendation, and the coming congregational meeting. I indicated to him that this was a process that, from the beginning was bathed in prayer, and that the process we had followed was in compliance with our congregation's by-laws. Moreover, I indicated that each step in the process was done in an atmosphere of as much spiritual discernment as we could muster. Following the review, I remarked, "Frankly, I have not been involved in a more responsible process. I can't help but feel that it has been blessed by our Lord and that the congregation's decision will be too." We agreed to disagree on that issue.

Then I addressed his remark. "You could stop this if you would!" "As you know," I remarked, "our church polity does not give me that kind of power. My role has been to aid in designing a process out of which the recommendation has grown. Even if I wanted to stop it, I could not legally do it. But let me add that I stand behind the decisions to this point. If the congregation approves the recommendation, I will stand behind that too, and we will begin the process of relocation. I'm very sorry that we have such disagreement on the issue and I am here to let you know that I care deeply for you and your wife, no matter our difference on the issue of relocation."

"I'll take your word for that, but know that if the decision is approved, we will be leaving the congregation." To which I responded, "I regret if it comes to that, but if that is your decision, then you have my blessing." Following a prayer, I departed.

The congregation approved the recommendation for relocation and from that point on, this individual did not attend Sunday worship again.

I was somewhat surprised that there was not more negative reaction from the congregation at large to his leaving; in fact, there were numerous remarks about how much more harmonious things had become in his absence. And I must confess that, while I felt a loss in his absence, there was a sprinkle of delight that I no longer had to deal with the tension he had been willing and able to create. Somehow, I sensed that my job would be a little easier now.

But the sense of loss was more real than that of relief.

Always, I have affirmed diversity of thought within the group—even when it is expressed so awkwardly as his. Some sense of personal failure gnawed at my conscience at not being able to reconcile him to the group's decision. What could have I have done differently that may have motivated him to get on board with our process? Thankfully, the story does not end here.

He did leave our congregation for another but he kept coming back for memorial services for his friends. That had always been one of his strengths— expressing care for people in their loss of loved ones.

After a memorial service for one of his friends, I noticed he lingered in the sanctuary after everyone else had departed. As I gathered my materials from the pulpit, I noticed he was walking toward me down the center aisle. I stepped from behind the pulpit and walked to the center of the chancel when I heard him say, "Jim may I have a moment of your time?" "Of course," I responded, as I left the chancel, to meet him in the aisle. As we approached one another, he opened his arms. I noticed he had some tears. I met his warm embrace and experienced the inspiration of his greeting, "Jim, I just wanted to say to you that you are a wonderful pastor and I love you." We just held each other and shed the tears of joy that—even when it seemed that we had lost our friendship, there was a spirit of mutual respect and spiritual brotherhood that transcended our disagreement.

He would continue with his new congregation and I with mine. But, for me, there was a pleasant sense of reunion of our spirits that continued to bless me until his death...and even now, as he continues in the community of the saints.

Along the way, we will encounter persons who will challenge us. My recommendation is that, while there are appropriate limits to be placed and observed, rejection of another person is not an option. Indeed, these folks may very well be those "extra grace required" people of whom my friend spoke. I am very grateful that the ethic of love called forth by the Great Commandment has freed me to have a relationship with those EGRs!

But there is more for which I have been set free when it comes to the ministry of reconciliation. This one has to do with celebrating my freedom to choose a more positive concept of justice than the traditional notion of justice as retribution.

4. Freedom to Affirm a More Positive Concept of Justice

According to Webster, justice is that principle of ideal of moral rightness (Equity) or conformity to moral rightness in conduct or attitude (Righteousness). This definition focuses primarily upon human to human relationships as in the case of affirming civil rights in a society where those have either not existed or have been taken away.

When placed in the context of Christian faith, justice includes, but expands that concept to focus upon humans in their relationship to God. In that case the more appropriate word is *justification,* that state of being set right in one's relationship to God, made possible by God's grace.

In short, justice may be thought of as that which reigns when wrongs have been made right.

Sharon Baker, focusing upon *types* of justice identifies two types prominent in our Judeo-Christian faith tradition, *retributive justice* and *restorative justice.6* By "retributive justice," she means that form of justice that puts things right through punishment or payback. This is represented in the law that stipulates "an eye for an eye." It does not require forgiveness. On the other hand, there is "restorative justice," also known as "reconciling justice" which occurs when one is reconciled with a guilty offender and the relationship is restored. This type of justice does require forgiveness.

The Bible, particularly the Old Testament, reflects both types of justice. In the social context the use of retributive justice seems more popular. This type of justice occurs when one has offended another and must pay the price to set the wrong right. In whatever way one has offended another, whether inflicting blindness or murder, that person must pay back—establish justice—through surrendering either his eye or his life.

At the time of Jesus' ministry in the first century, retributive justice reigned, particularly in prominent Pharisaic legalism. For example, there is the case of a woman who had been discovered committing adultery. The Pharisees brought her to the Temple to which Jesus had gone to teach. They brought her into his presence where they presented her case, saying: "'Teacher...this woman was caught in the very act of committing adultery. In our Law of Moses (it is) commanded that such a woman must be stoned to death. Now, what do you say?' They said this to trap Jesus...." (John 8:5-6--NRSV).

The Pharisees know the Law and they intend to stone the woman in obedience to that law. Their presenting her to Jesus and asking for his judgment on the matter is a step in their plan to place him in a position of playing his justice card in such a way that he would become vulnerable to their accusations.

Jesus also knows their Law and, as they interpret it, he knows that it requires her death by stoning. What does he do? John tells us that he bent over and wrote something on the ground with his finger. The Jesus looked at the Pharisees and said, "Whichever one of you has committed no sin may throw the first stone at her.... When they heard this, they all left, one by one, the older ones first" (vss.7-8—Today's English Version).

Now picture this. Once the Pharisees had left, Jesus

is standing alone with the woman: "He (Jesus) straightened up and said to her, 'Where are they? Is there no one left to condemn you?' 'No one, sir,' she answered. 'Well, then,' Jesus said, 'I do not condemn you either. Go, but do not sin again'" (vss. 10,11—TEV).

This story illustrates the difference in *retributive* and *restorative* justice. The Pharisees wanted retribution which called for the penalty of the Law to be applied through stoning the woman to death. Forgiveness is not an option. Death by stoning is the logical conclusion of their punitively oriented legalism. On the other hand, motivated by God's love ethic, Jesus wanted restoration which called for holding her accountable for her sin, and, in the same measure, forgiving her and directing her to put a stop to her promiscuity.

Experiences like this one had convinced Jesus that religious legalism, as the name suggests, gives priority to the law; not to the person who has broken the law. But Jesus gave priority to the persons who were perceived to have broken the law. It was his conviction that persons, created in the image of God, should take precedence over the law which had been created to manage human beings. Thus, in another incident, in face of Pharisaical accusation that on the Sabbath his hungry disciples had broken the law by collecting some grain to eat, thus breaking the Sabbath requirement of fasting, Jesus declared: "The Sabbath was made for humankind, not humankind for the Sabbath; so, the Son of Man is lord even of the Sabbath...." (Mark 2:27-28—T.E.V.)

When the Pharisees asked him to identify the greatest of the commandments, freed from legalism, Jesus referenced the "Great Commandment," to love God with our whole being and to love our neighbor as we love ourselves; thus, reminding his inquisitors and us that to live by the ethic of love is the ultimate fulfillment of God's holy will.

For Jesus legalism was just too restrictive, too punitive; too insensitive to the humanity of the offender. It was a system not compatible with his understanding of what it means to be faithful to God, thus, he used that occasion to declare a new paradigm for ethical living: the ethics of love which places its focus upon restorative or reconciling justice.

We have just described what retributive justice looks like in its social context. Let's expand that focus to include our relationship with God. The Bible is full of incidents that illustrate the popularity of retributive justice thought to be utilized by God in relationship to people. Indeed, the story we have just considered—the woman caught in the act of adultery is a carry over into the New Testament of Old Testament practice, the implication being that God has given us a law by which to be governed, one which requires retribution for wrong acts in order to establish justice. Since God was construed to have given the law, by implication, it is God who requires retribution.

Israel was born in and developed among the cultures of the Middle East where she was located, where the Old Testament takes place. Those cultures functioned by the laws of retribution and retaliation. Violence was a way of life. Justice was established through violent means. The people were saturated in that way of dealing with misconduct. It was so much a part of their thinking that even God was perceived to think and behave in that fashion. As a result, they seemed not to have much concern about invading an enemy city and slaying all its inhabitants, including women and children, and doing that in the name of God.

We can learn from this that, regardless of the period in which one may live, including our own, we have a tendency to "baptize" our violence, i.e., to interpret *our* violent ways as the way of *God*.

Behind the rationale of wickedness, wicked people have perpetrated wicked things in the name of God. Whether it be revenge hangings done in the name of justice in the old south, cross burnings by the KKK, or massacres like the one at Me Lai during the Vietnam War. Such cases represent a human tendency to choose a cause, any cause, about which they feel strongly and give it divine sanction in order to justify its violence against other human beings or even against the natural world of creation.

In her book, *Razing Hell*, Sharon Baker encourages us to read scripture through what she calls "the lens of Jesus." Jesus' commitment to restorative or reconciling justice—as in the case of the woman caught in the act of adultery—helps us to look at our faith history with its distinctive strands of retributive and restorative justice and choose the latter in hope that healing may occur rather than punishment.

For example, the book of Ezekiel contains both strands of justice. In chapter 7 the Lord declares the end of Israel and describes in ghoulish detail how its people will be punished and slaughtered. However, in chapter 37, Israel is pictured as a valley of dry bones. The Lord beholds the scene and declares his intention to reconnect those dry bones, grow skin and muscle, and induce breath so that they become, again, living beings, restored to greatness. Why? Because God has made a covenant of eternal love with them. Early in the book of Habakkuk, the Lord, in very tough terms condemns the Jewish people but, in the end, declares his love for them until they return to him.

Commenting on these as examples of God's restorative justice, Richard Rohr declares: "God always outdoes the Israelites' sin by loving them even more." (Rohr., p. 184)

There is no escaping the fact, however, that there are multiple examples of retributive justice throughout the Bible; particular in the Old Testament. Do I believe that God commands the murder of women and children to serve the cause of justice? As I look at those through the "lens of Jesus" I conclude that the voice our ancient ancestors heard speaking those orders was not the voice of God.

Unless one holds the view that the scriptures are the result of a mechanical process in which God dictated literal words to biblical secretaries who wrote exactly what God said, the exact words of God which now come to us on the pages of Holy Scripture, so that every word is God's, to view the radical examples of retributive justice as having been ordered by God becomes problematic. On the other hand, if one views scripture to be the written record of those who wrote about their inspiring experience with God and expressed their conclusions in their own words, she or he is able to realize that some of their conclusions may very well be interpreted as projections of imperfect human beings who could have mistakenly attributed to God things that God did not actually declare. So, as one reads Holy Scripture through the "lens of Jesus" one can detect such dynamic and evaluate it.

The larger point of this discussion, however, is to say that justice can be perceived in retributive terms (God's wrath inflicting violent punishment for wrongdoing) or in restorative, reconciling terms (non-violent discipline from a loving Father designed to lead the offender to the point of receiving God's forgiveness and having his or her life restored).

When I view the issue through the "lens of Jesus" I am led to the conclusion that, choosing to love folk into reconciliation with God, Jesus did not inflict violent punishment upon folks; neither does God, nor should we.

For me, to experience these conclusions is freeing, indeed. And I owe that freedom to Jesus' Great Commandment in which he reminds us that God's way is the way of love and restoration, not violence and destruction. I believe it is this conviction that stands behind his declaration that on the commandment to love God and others hang all the law and the prophets. In other words, the way of love is the foundational essence of the life of faithful service to God.

This consideration of distinguishing between retributive and restorative justice leads me to bring it to bear upon Jesus' death. Why did he die? And, did he die because God demanded it? On the other hand, could it be that his death was the result of Satan's demand for a ransom? Or was it the religious and civil establishment that demanded it? What is behind Jesus' death and what does his death mean? This question brings us into the vicinity of the justice issue.

There are various traditional explanations for the purpose of Jesus' death. Here are some of the most popular: (1) His death was demanded by God as a way of upholding the holiness of God, i.e., a price had to be paid for the sin of the world if God was going to be able to forgive, Jesus' death was the price to be paid. (2) Jesus' death was the ransom demanded by Satan in order to release people from his grasp and give them back to God. (3) His death was a result of the hostilities of both the religious and political establishments in Israel who considered Jesus to be a deep threat to their security. (4) God allowed the death of his son as a way of convincing the world of the depth of divine love.

I have problems with first two of these. Number 1 views God as demanding the death of the son as the price to be paid to meet the demands of God's justice. I think this view places God in a very bad light, as one whose holiness cannot be upheld unless there is an enormous price paid to defend it, namely, the violent death of God's own son, an arrangement in which Jesus ends up protecting us from God! I have difficulty with this distorted perception of God's nature, for at its center God's true nature is pure love whose strategy is to love creation into reconciliation with the Divine. The efficacy of love in doing this is made clearer in my response to number 4. Moreover, the idea that God demands the Son's death in order to release God's vast resources of forgiveness, implies that God is cruel, stingy and stubborn.

In short, option number 1 places God in the retributive justice arena as God is perceived to demand violence and death as payment for our imperfection.

I also have difficulty with number 2 which views Jesus' death as a ransom payment to Satan in order to "buy us back" from sin and evil. Obviously, this gives more power to Satan and diminishes the glory of God, a theory that in my view is not compatible with the Judeo-Christian conviction that God, our Creator and Sustainer, is greater than anything or anyone else. The extremely mundane tone of option 2 is offensive to my spiritual sensitivity. Then why do so many seem to choose options 1 and 2? I believe that one of the issues is the language of "sacrifice" and "ransom" used in the Scriptures.

These words and the concepts behind them were popular in the general Middle Eastern culture and in Judaism during the first century. It is not unusual that both the words and concepts would be uncritically "borrowed" by some of the biblical writers.

I suggest we look beyond specific words to the deeper and more profound theological implications of God's mercy and grace, God's compassion and love. In other words, look at the issues through the "lens of Jesus."

Option number 3 has merit as a partial explanation for Jesus' death. My reading of the circumstances surrounding his death indicates that the profound effectiveness of Jesus' ministry was such a threat to both the religious and political establishment of his day that those establishments lashed out in self-defense. But I find in option 3 no theological rationale for Jesus' death—only a political one. In other words, it has accuracy as far as it goes, but it does not go far enough to get to the heart of the theological/spiritual dimensions of Jesus' passion.

Option number 4 comes closest to satisfying my mind and spirit regarding the cause of Jesus' death. In my view, based on my understanding of God from Holy Scripture, God's track-record of involvement in human history and the history of the natural world, along with the experience of God in my own life, God's justice is not retributive but restorative and reconciling. In the final analysis, I believe that God's judgment is *always* designed to bring God's creation back into a positive relationship. The greatest force for doing that is not punishment either now or hereafter, but pure love that is the very essence of God.

In that context I share the following story:

I cannot remember the teller's name but the story was told during a sermon in the Benton Chapel at Vanderbilt University. It continues to inspire me. It's about a college student who is so enamored with rationalism and science that he decides to challenge the religious establishment. He proceeds to a church, asking to see the pastor. Warmly received, he is ushered to the pastor's study where he is greeted by a priest. As soon as they are seated, the young man presents his point: "Sir, I am here to request that you reflect upon your role in perpetuating the vast sea of superstition that surrounds us. If you and others will abandon your participation in this tradition, society's progress to new levels of intellectual credibility will be enhanced."

The elderly priest listened without interruption. When the young man paused from presenting his case, the priest responded, "I am glad that you have come and I hear what you are saying." Without entering any kind of a defensive apology, the priest proceeded to ask, "Will you do something for me? To which the young man responded, "Sir, you have received me warmly and have listened politely. What is it you want of me?"

"Come with me to our place of worship," said the priest.

"Show me the way," replied the student.

Together they proceeded to the place of corporate worship, a large area surrounded by multicolored stained glass and other religious symbolism. Everything in the space--the glass, the other symbols, and the architecture—funneled attention toward a large crucifix hanging above the altar. For a moment they both stood silent before the scene. Then the priest made his request. Speaking softly, he said, "Please go forward, stand at the foot of the steps to the altar, look up at the Crucifix and say, "Christ died for me."

Without any detectable hesitation, the young man agreed and stridently made his way to the area, looked up at the cross and declared, "Christ died for me and I don't give a damn!" Immediately, returning to the priest, he said, "There, it's done!"

The priest asked, "Will you do it again?"

The student returned to the scene, again looked up at the cross and declared, "Christ died for me and I couldn't care less!"

Will you do it another time?" asked the priest, softly.

This time the student appeared less strident. As he arrived and looked up, he froze into an awkward silence; then began to utter, haltingly, "Christ… died…for…me…" followed by falling to his knees, sobbing.

The priest ran to embrace him. As he took the young man in his arms, he heard him pray, "O God, forgive me, I have been such a fool. I yield before your love."

This story reached deeply into my heart when I

heard it years ago, and continues to stir my emotion with its ability to sharpen my sense of God's magnetic love. Whether, at any given moment my resistance to growth is inordinate pride or despair, the love of God communicating with me through the crucifixion event continues to pull me from the poisonous tentacles of human frailty toward freedom and wholeness.

When I look at the cross, I do not presume to understand all its mystery, but because of the magnetic love it radiates, I feel a pull into the very heart of the Divine because I am convinced that the Divine heart is one of love and acceptance, not wrath and rejection. I am convinced that whatever the depth of the mystery—a mystery whose essence lies beyond my limited comprehension— that the cross is not designed for God to change God's mind about us—for God has always and will always love us. Rather, the cross is a symbol that calls us to change our minds about God, that God is not a violent, ruthless, dictator, but is our God, our Savior, our Lover, the One who has always and will always be for us and not against us.

Is it any wonder, then, that when confronted by the Pharisees with the request that he identify the greatest of the commandments, Jesus offers a persuasive, transforming insight about the essential point of faith and of our walk in faith: "'You shall love the Lord your God with all your heart, and with all your soul and with all your mind.' This is the first and greatest commandment. And a second is like it: 'You shall love your neighbor as yourself.' On these two commandments hang all the law and the prophets" (Matthew 22:37-40).

Let's prepare, now, to consider a final implication of living by Jesus' ethic of love.

5. Freedom to Face the Future with Hope

By now you are aware that I grew up in a culture heavily influenced with the Bible. Church played a central role in my life. On Sunday there were Sunday school and Worship. Sunday evening began with Youth Group and continued into Sunday Evening Worship. When Wednesday rolled around it was back to church for Bible Study.

My experience of such religious saturation, in many ways was a positive one. For as long as I can remember my mind respected God, my heart loved God while, in some dimensions of both, I feared God, all rooted in my experience with the orientation of our congregation. As I look back on those days, I am aware that considerable and genuine love lay at the center of our congregation's life, especially for its children and youth. When I went to church I was surrounded with people, both men and women, of all ages who adored me. Rarely did I feel ignored. For the most part hugs, kisses, embraces, words of encouragement and other expressions of adoration came my way.

When I went away to college, the volume of these expressions reduced from a river to a creek, but they were still there. I remember, for example, Uncle Bill Thurman—an uncle not by blood but by affection—wrote regularly to me to let me know he was thinking of (and praying for) me. At break time, when I returned to my community and my church participation, I was always met with open arms from many people who seemed genuinely interested in the quality of my college experience. To this day, when I return to this still-thriving congregation, though there are fewer people I know, I still experience the warmth of those with whom I have a history. No doubt, my life would be considerably less blessed had I not experienced my congregation and its loving people.

However, I must say that not all my experience there was positive. For example, the orientation of the congregation's theology—in many ways the theology also of the wider community and culture—left me with a vision of the future that felt to me, particularly with the passing of the years, quite pessimistic and negative.

I remember, as a young person, thinking that the world was filled with considerably more wickedness than righteousness. Some of my most beloved Christian education teachers contributed to my negativity; particularly in their massive doses of theological doom, beginning with their conviction that soon after its creation, the world, because of the act of Adam and Eve eating from the tree of the knowledge of good and evil, experienced a great fall into sin which left every one without virtue, stained to the core, evil in nature, and depraved beyond any ability to reflect goodness. As a result, I remember that one of the most prominent assessments of my world was the conclusion that it was "going to Hell in a handbasket." I was taught, too, that Christ's sole purpose in coming was to save us from such depravity and destruction by offering himself as a bloody sacrifice in order to appease a very angry God whose wrath could be turned away only through such a sacrifice and our belief in its purpose. Somewhere I picked up a huge amount of insecurity—even in that "saving" arrangement—that left me wondering whether "when the roll is called up yonder, I'll be there;" if so, only by the hair of my chin as I squeaked through St. Peter's vetting process and under the watchful eye of an angry God.

The future? As my young mind projected into the future there were prominent and very threatening indications that the evil which already existed in abundance would only grow more prevalent and intense until such time—by God's own calculation—Jesus Christ would return to call all of us up before his judgment bar.

I remember, well, how I fine-tuned my ear for the "sound of the trumpet" which would announce his coming. For example, when I was around the age of 13, my beloved brother, Eddie, and I had a habit of going to the Saturday movie matinee at the movie theatre in Elk Park, a larger community about 5 miles from our home in Heaton. The cost of admission was 25 cents. To get popcorn and a coke was another 20 cents. Eddie and I would load up on both, find ourselves on the right side of the theatre about half way toward the front and, from there, relax to enjoy the likes of Hopalong Cassidy, Lash Larue, Roy Rogers, Clyde Beatty, and others. As I remember, these were all "safe" characters. The plot of their releases was always an illustration of good versus evil, with good always coming out on top (which sometimes felt strange in light of my theological bent toward the doom that was eminent in the world, given the power of evil over the good).

I remember several occasions, as I watched the screen, I would break away from the near-captivating presentation, and listen for the "sound of the trumpet" thinking, If the Lord comes back while I am watching this movie will my chances of passing his inspection be considerably reduced? As I weighed the issue, I remember thinking that, indeed, my chances could be reduced. In the back of my mind were still vestiges of a deeply moralistic—puritanical in many ways—culture which took the position that going to the movies, like participating in dancing, was worldly and sinful; that movies had a way of taking our attention from a vigilant watch for the second coming preceded by the Gabriel's piercing trumpet blare. Though I experienced such ambivalence, I continued to go to movies, willing to take the chance that I was O.K. in the long run. After all my religious denomination was slightly more liberal on such issues than so many of the other religious groups that took a much more rigid stance.

If you remember earlier in this book, I referenced my experience of going away to Bible College and beginning a process of working through some of the implications of my religious upbringing. You may remember, too, that I eventually became critical of the theology of my heritage and began, fervently, to seek alternative ways of understanding and living out the Christian faith.

That alternative turned out to be a life-saving and transformative experience. It impacted, my negativity and pessimism, providing a much more positive image of God, the world around me, and the destiny of all creation.

That transformation began with a reevaluation of the status of creation. Earlier, I had believed it to be totally depraved because of the so-called Fall precipitated by the disobedient act of Adam and Eve. From the same book, *Genesis*, I would come to learn from the creation stories that God called creation "good" five times (1:1-22) and "very good" in 1:31.

From early in my memory I had heard folk talking

about Original Sin and how we were all tainted with it through inheritance from the act of disobedience by Adam and Eve. I learned, however, that the positive flow of the story's emphasis of goodness in Genesis 1, took a very negative turn when fourth-century Christian theologian, Augustine shifted the focus from Genesis 1 to the darker vision of Genesis 3 with its emphasis upon the first sin and banishment of Adam and Eve from the Garden of Eden.

Augustine's writings had a heavy influence upon the direction of Christian theology for centuries to come, shifting our focus away from the inherent goodness of the natural world, including humans, and replacing it with the disastrous implications of the doctrine of Original Sin.

Theologian Richard Rohr focuses upon some of the consequences of Augustine's shifting focus, particularly its implications for what he calls "The Primacy of Christ." Rohr believes that, as a result of Augustine's negative valuation, the fuller meaning of Jesus Christ, our Savior, was shrunk so that he became "a mere Johnny-come-lately 'answer 'to the problem of sin." 8

In this observation, Rohr is not implying that Jesus has nothing to do with solving the problem of sin. He is, however, emphasizing that the wider profound nature and role of Jesus is lost in that dominant original sin imagery, with its many implications. As a result, "his (Jesus') death, rather than his life, was defined as saving us." 9

This development toward negative valuation of God's creation; particularly the depravity implied in Augustine's doctrine of Original Sin, reminds me of a popular theory of atonement that began to emerge, namely, the so called "satisfaction theory" which held that Christ's bloody and violent sacrifice on the cross was demanded by God in order for God to be 'satisfied' and to change God's mind about us, in order to extend forgiveness to us.

Deeper implications grew out of the Augustinian way of thinking. For example, a popular view arose—we still hear echoes of it—which held that, even with Jesus' death on the Cross—the world grows more and more wicked so that, eventually, it must be destroyed by the hand of God who will, in turn, send a large portion of humanity to Hell. A Hell where the wicked will be punished by burning which will last forever. Ordinarily, when we think of something thrown into the fire, we think of its being consumed. Not so in Hell's case. As Dante's *Inferno* makes clear, the body will not be consumed but will constantly be renewed so that the tortuous burning can last forever and ever. With this pessimistic assessment of the world, its peoples and its future, dominating my thinking during my younger years, I remember occasions when looking into an intense fire like that in my grandmother's fireplace or at pictures of Pittsburgh's steel mills with their blasting furnaces and thinking, my goodness that would be horrible! I remember also asking myself, "given God's loving nature why would God allow such things as that?!"

Thankfully, my spiritual journey found an alternative way of assessing the world and its destiny, and significantly, the larger role of Jesus as the Christ than that of a victim of a bloody sacrifice.

At the core of my faith is a commitment to the concept that, from the very beginning, faith, hope and love are deep within our nature. Not only do we have the Genesis emphasis upon creation's inherent goodness, we have other biblical evidence. Take, for example, Paul, in Romans 5:5, speaking of hope, declares: "...and hope does not disappoint us, because God's love has been poured into our hearts...." Later, in chapter 8, he writes: "When we cry, 'Abba, Father!' it is that very spirit (the Spirit of God within us) bearing witness with our spirit that we are the children of God...(vss.15-16).

Throughout Holy Scripture, God's love for creation including human beings, is never lost. God, our creator, knows our value, sees God's own image in us, and is determined to honor that value and image by leading us to our intended destiny.

The coming of Jesus as the Christ, caught the world's attention. His entire life was an adventure in displaying God's love in unmistakable ways. Both his words and deeds embraced the world and its peoples, reminding all that the foundation of all reality is God, whose being is an inexhaustible fountain of love and acceptance. It was he who taught us about a Father who refused to reject his returning Prodigal Son, blind persons whose sight he restored, adulterers whom he forgave, and foreigners whom he embraced. He taught, and became, the way of love, teaching legalistic Pharisees that religion is not essentially about rules and regulations and doctrines, but was about loving God and our neighbor. Like a beautiful symphony, Jesus' life reached a dramatic, cosmos–moving crescendo when he submitted to the cross—pure love hanging on a tree—and finally cried out with his last breath, "It is finished!"

Reflecting upon his life and his death, I am aware that Jesus' saving work began with his ministry and continued through the events of his life, finally expressing itself in the drama of his Passion. He was always our Savior from beginning to end, drawing us to God and to one another as nothing else could or can. In that process, near the end, he reflected the potential that God has placed within all human beings; declaring: "I am telling you the truth: those who believe in me will do what I do—yes, they do even greater things..." (John 14:12—TEV).

The essence of Christ's saving work began in showing us the life we are capable of living—a life of love for God and others—and continued all the way through the cross in a display of love that got the world's attention. That life had such powerful effect that, everywhere, folk began to be drawn through it to move beyond their blindness to our true nature so that we could recognize that we are, after all, the children of God.

The life to which Christ calls us—we call it the Christian life—is in very simple terms becoming who we are. Consider these:

1 John 3:1-2 (TEV)— "See how much the Father has loved us! His love is so great that we are called God's children—and so, in fact, we are...we are now God's children, but it is not yet clear what we shall become. But we know that when Christ appears, we shall be like him, because we shall see him as he really is."

11 Peter 1:3-4 (TEV)— "God's divine power has given us everything we need to live a truly religious life through our knowledge of the one who called us to share in his own glory and goodness. In this way he has given us the very great, and precious gifts he promised, so that by means of those gifts, you may escape from the destructive lust that is in the world, and may come to share the divine nature."

This divine nature, Richard Rohr calls our "core identity," and defines our task: "...we have to awaken, allow, and advance this core identity by saying a conscious yes to it and (by) drawing upon it as a reliable and Absolute Source...*image* must become *likeness*." 10

Thank God, Original Goodness trumps Original Sin! Jesus life and death combined to remove the blinders to this great truth about ourselves and creation.

To say it another way, there is a lot of goodness in the world and in us folks!! From the beginning God has recognized that what is needed is for us to *awaken* to it. His most effective instrument for awakening us to that goodness is Jesus as the Christ.

Millions across the globe are awakening to that, saying yes to Christ and getting together with God who is leading, not just humanity, but all creation to its destiny. That destiny was emphasized at creation when everyone and everything was in perfect harmony with God. The very term "*Garden of Eden*" conveys that peaceful imagery. But, somewhere along the way we lost our way. The vision, so clear in creation, became blurred, so God began to work effectively for its restoration and while not total there, its reality is coming!

Early on, I felt that God's work in Jesus as the Christ, was to gather a *few* of us (since his way is *narrow*) and take us away to heaven. Moreover, I felt that our primary purpose in being cooperative with God was to get ourselves into heaven.

Shifting our focus somewhat, let me state that somewhere along the journey, I discovered more, equally rich, insights that related to such issues as that for which Christ "saves" us (Are we saved to save our own skin, or for more?), the volume of those who share the freedom of being led to our destiny (are just a few of us going to make it or is the number much larger?), and the location of that destiny (are we being carried by the Divine to some distant "heaven" or is the destination nearer?) Of course, Jesus is saving us for our sake! It seems perfectly normal for us to want him to save us. But the focus of Christ's salvation is far broader than just ourselves as individuals, and in such a way that it appears that we are saved in order to see that God wants that for everyone, and that we are called to become co-workers with God in sharing that good news to the entire world so that others may begin to see and become who they are, namely, children of God.

I emphasize this point not only for its truth, but for its relevance for a time many of whose people of faith seem to be yearning for their "personal" salvation. Metaphorically, it seems to me, we seem to go running wildly to God—maybe even pushing and shoving others out of the way—in order to get our name written in the "Lamb's Book of Life" (a listing of all those who belong to God). That settled, others may come as they wish, *after us.*

It seems that a more faithful metaphor would be millions awakening to the Good News of the Gospel, a process in which we find ourselves acting as spiritual mid-wives aiding others to experience renewed sight and insight.

As I understand Jesus, his emphasis is expressed best, not in terms of some spiritual selfishness, but in terms of self-giving: "Those who try to gain their own life will lose it; but those who lose their life for my sake will gain it" (Matthew 10:39—TEV).

In light of all this, it seems to me that Christ has brought you and me into the light that we may join him in bringing others into the light who, in turn, will join him in bringing others. It grows and grows, exponentially, until light has completely overcome the darkness.

This leads me to consider the number of those who are being "saved, "restored", "enlightened." It may not surprise you that I do not have an exact number. What I do know, however, is that God desires everyone's salvation (2 Peter 3:9—TEV). If that is God's desire its accomplishment is surely within the realm of possibility. But the idea of Hell hoists its halting hand as if to say, "Wait a minute! What do you think I am for?" Consider it, is Hell not that concept of a place to which many will go because they have not been willing to hear the good news that they are accepted (and forgiven) by God?

I am struck by the number of scholars questioning the concept of Hell as it has come to us so dramatically through the imagination of Dante's *Inferno*. For the most part biblical and theological scholars are emphasizing a need for us to distinguish between much of that which has come to us through our wider culture about Hell and the concept as it is dealt with in Holy Scripture.

In this connection I am thinking of the work done by Sharon L. Baker. Let me identify her for you: She is Assistant Professor of Theology and Religion and Coordinator of the Peace and Conflict Studies Program at Messiah College in Grantham, Pennsylvania. She has published numerous articles and speaks frequently throughout the United Sates on nonviolent atonement and hell. A former stay-at-home mom, Baker received her PhD from Southern Methodist University in 2006 and is the mother of four grown boys. Earlier I referenced her book, *Razing Hell*, published in 2010. There she offers a rethinking of traditional views of hell. Cautioning us to resist much of our culture's thinking on the subject, she makes her case from the Bible itself.

In her view, the Bible does not teach of hell as a place to which wicked folk go, there to be tortured for eternity. She clarifies for the reader that, in the Bible, fire is thought of as God's purifying element which separates the chaff from the wheat. Fire, therefore, in biblical terms is more in line with the theory of *restorative* (reconciling) justice as opposed to *retributive* (punishing) justice. From the Holy Scriptures she makes the case that there are consequences to resisting God's grace so beautifully expressed in the life and death of

Jesus; that fire is the future of those who do resist, but the fire is not conceptualized as a punishing and eternal fire in which such people will burn forever, rather God's instrument of purification and restoration that "burns away" the resistance in order to restore, reconcile, and save. While I do not have room to do an exhaustive description of Baker's thought, I do recommend for those of you interested in the subject, the acquisition of her book as well as a couple of other works, Jon Sweeny's *Inventing Hell* (New York: Jericho Books, 2014) and Julie Ferwerda's, *Raising Hell: Christianity's Most Controversial Doctrine Put Under Fire* (Lander WY. Vagabond Group, 2011).

Particularly, Baker resists the aura of retributive justice that so surrounds and permeates much of the traditional thinking about Hell. However, she feels that such perception of God goes beyond being *distasteful* to being *unbiblical* in that it views God as committed to getting even with those who have not been cooperative in God's graceful efforts and, in the end, is perceived as resorting to eternal punishment. That, in her thinking, misrepresents the biblical conversation about the meaning of "fire," "Gehenna," and the like.

Baker's insights have implications, of course, for the number of people who will end up in Heaven. For her, the amazing grace of God and God's provision of restorative justice for purposes of reconciling, will result in the salvation of all those who respond positively to God's restorative, reconciling justice. For those who are not restored through that process the alternative, in her thought, is not eternal punishment but total annihilation, as in separation from reality. Scripture's reference to God's will that "none should perish but that all should come to everlasting life," therefore, serves as a positive warning that God who, as Creator and Savior, is heavily invested in the natural world, including humans, and will not lose. Piggybacking on this biblical idea of God's ultimate victory in saving the world—not just a portion of it—Rob Bell in 2001 wrote his remarkable book, *Love Wins* (Harper One), a book about Heaven, Hell, and the fate of every person who ever lived.

This gift of Heaven, is it to be handed to us only at the **end** of our lives here on earth?

As a youngster, that was my view: When we reach the end of our lives here, we die and go to heaven. Now, there is an element of truth in that view, I believe. I think the Apostle Paul was making that point when he wrote: "Now we look forward with confidence to our heavenly bodies, realizing that every moment we spend in these earthly bodies is time spent away from our eternal home in heaven with Jesus….we are not afraid, but are quite content to die, for then we will be at home with the Lord" (2 Corinthians 5:6-8—The Living Bible paraphrased).

One morning I went to the hospital to visit one

of my parishioners who was actively dying from cancer. He was a prominent physician in our community and a person of faith. As I turned the corner into his room his emaciated face lit up as he exclaimed, "Oh, Jim, I am so glad you are here, I have something wonderful to tell you."

"I'm all ears," Gene, I responded.

He continued, "Look over there at the wall of my room. Earlier this morning it became a stage with those long curtains and they were closed. When I first saw it, I wondered about its meaning. Then, an arm pulled back part of the curtain and a person stepped out in front. Immediately I recognized that it was Jesus. He looked at me and said, 'Gene it's almost time for me to come for you and I just want to show up a little early and show you what is waiting for you.' Then, he pulled the curtains completely open and I can tell you that I have never witnessed a more beautiful scene in my entire life, so beautiful that it is beyond my description."

"What did it mean to you?" I asked.

"Jim, it was a picture of Heaven and I believe that at the end of my life here, Jesus wanted to give me this inspirational assurance of the place to which I am going."

We rejoiced together, then prayed a prayer of thanksgiving, after which we called his wife who brought the 10 and 12-year-old sons to hear dad's

Journeying Forward Toward Spiritual Freedom

story. After he had repeated the vision to the sons, he asked, "Do you understand what this means boys?" Both nodded their heads affirmatively. The entire family—as well as the pastor—sensed the meaning. Gene would soon leave us and we had been blessed by his vision of his destination.

So, yes, our faith anticipates an experience called Heaven which will become a *full* realization at the end of our lives, but notice I have emphasized the word "full," and for a reason. The reason is based on a promise Jesus made that we *begin* our experience of heaven earlier than the time of our death: "I am telling you the truth: those who hear my words and believe in him who sent me have eternal life. They will not be judged, but have *already* passed from death to life" (John 5:24—TEV). This point, put in the context of loving others, is reiterated in 1 John 3:14--TEV: "We know that have left death and come over into life; we know it because we love others. Those who do not love are still under the power of death."

As I understand it, the message is this: Our experience of heaven begins at the point of our reconciliation with God through our Lord, Jesus Christ when we are given the gift to love God and others and to be loved by them. Our heavenly gift continues to build and build so that when we die it bursts forth into full bloom.

How broadly is the gift of heaven to be shared among

God's creation? You may be thinking that the gift of heaven (as complete reconciliation and restoration with God) is just for *human beings*, as though, somehow, only we humans, out of all the species of plants and animals, are chosen for this fortuitous blessing. This would be a mistaken interpretation according to Holy Scripture. Consider, for example, the insights offered by the Apostle Paul in his *Letter to the Romans:*

> I consider that what we suffer at this present time cannot be compared at all with the glory that is going to be revealed to us. *All of creation* waits with eager longing for God to reveal his children. For creation was condemned to lose its purpose.... Yet there was this hope that *creation itself* would one day be set free from slavery to decay and would share the glorious freedom of the children of God. For we know that up to the present time *all of creation* groans with pain, like the pain of childbirth. But it is not just creation alone which groans; we who have the Spirit as the first of God's gifts also groan within ourselves as we wait for God to make us his children and set the whole being free (8:18-23—TEV).

Here, Paul reveals his awareness of the important foundational block the stories of creation play in the development of Judeo-Christian faith. God loved and loves all of it—not just humans—and the power of redemption promises to restore all of creation—including humans—to the peace and harmony for which they were originally created.

Redemption seems always to be holistic. Its target is not just a section or a sliver of creation, but the whole.

In tandem with that thought, let's now move to consider that the "place" of heaven is ultimately to be our good earth. Jesus had hinted at this arrangement when, in the prayer he taught us, directed us to pray "...thy will be done on *earth* as it is in *heaven*." The *Book of Revelation* becomes explicit when it reaches its *eschatological* (having to do with last things) crescendo in chapter 21:

> Then I saw a new heaven and a new earth. The first heaven and the first earth disappeared, and the sea vanished. And I saw the Holy City, the New Jerusalem, coming down out of heaven from God, prepared and ready, like a bride dressed to meet her husband. I heard a loud voice speaking from the throne: 'Now God's home is with people. He will live with them, and they shall be his people. God himself will be with them, and he will be their God. He will wipe away all tears from their eyes. There will be no more death, no more grief or crying or pain. The old things have disappeared.
>
> Then the one who sits on the throne said, 'And now I make all things new! 'He also said to me, write this, because these words are true and can be trusted' (Revelation 21:1-5—TEV).

One of John's points is to declare the ultimate "location" of heaven. He is quite explicit in declaring the message of his vision, namely, that Heaven, God's dwelling place, is to be in the midst of God's beloved creation.

The vision seems to suggest that things will have gone full circle when God restores things to the stage of perfection that was intended from the beginning.

Rob Bell puts it this way: "*Here* is the new *there*." 11

In summation, I have attempted to share my journey toward spiritual freedom. The catalyst for this movement is Jesus' encounter with the Pharisees resulting in his teaching that the essence of faithful living is to love God with our whole being and to love our neighbor as ourselves. It's a call to live by the ethic of love which enables us to be free from the restrictions so often imposed by the shadow side of our human nature, as well as the religious establishment whose definition of religion as a belief system is restrictive.

While, ideally, our following in Christ's way is not motivated by the rewards it brings, there are, nevertheless, rewards a plenty which begin to be shared at the outset of our journey of trusting God and are given in full measure at the end; not just to me and mine but to all who walk upon the path by loving God and others. And not just for us human beings, but for all God's creation.

In the beginning God invested heavily in all that God made. At the end, God's risk proves to be worth it all.

Journeying Forward Toward Spiritual Freedom

CONCLUSION

In this book I have acknowledged that there is a movement afoot in our culture that may be described, accurately, as "journeying toward spiritual freedom." That movement represents a drift away from institutional religion, perceived by some as too restrictive as well as largely irrelevant, and toward what is referred to as "spirituality," presumed to have less baggage and a significantly increased relevance in meeting the felt needs of a society that seems filled but unfulfilled,

In some important ways I agree with the conclusion of the above description and can understand the stated motivation of many who are rushing away from institutional religion. For me, however, some yellow flags appear. I have questions that need further exploration. For example, what are the implications for those of us who continue to experience a real sense of the sacred through our *institutional* experience? Is there a probability that some have given up on the institution too soon, without testing its potential for reform? What needs to change within the religious institution in order for participants to find adequate fulfillment? Are there elements in the institution, the loss of which would minimize our faith experience? Must one be either "religious" or "spiritual? Is there room— and a need—for both? Can lines of communication between "religionists" and "spiritualists" be established to explore whether, indeed, the two may be complementary under the appropriate circumstances or, forever, are they destined to become irreconcilable adversaries?

My hope is that these questions will be explored in such a way that an atmosphere of mutual respect will be created in which proponents of both approaches can come together. Aristotle described the space between two alternatives as the "golden mean" which suggests a rich vein of meaning to be found in a synthesis of the alternatives into something fresh and new, hence the *golden* mean. Often, we moderns describe it as a compromise that recognizes the assets and liabilities of the alternatives but, building upon their mutual desire to get to the truth of a matter, the opposing sides come together to explore the possibility of discovering the new and the better.

In a recent article Dr. L. Timothy Smith, President of Johnson University, writes about the mission of the Christian College. He quotes from Arthur F. Holmes' classic work on Christian higher education, *The Idea of a Christian College,* which declares that Christian education "should be a liberating experience that enlarges horizons, deepens insight, sharpens the mind, and sensitizes our ability to appreciate the good and the beautiful as well as the true." From there Dr. Smith continues in his own words: "On the other hand, there must be a good purpose for the liberation. Students must be trained toward a worthy goal for their education. Both dimensions are essential to a comprehensive Christian philosophy of education. (Now, here is what I want to highlight with italics in Smith's quote) *"Liberation without direction produces an open-mindedness that can lead to empty-headedness; direction without liberation fosters a doctrinaire traditionalism and ensnares students into the limited scope of their own cultural vision."* 1

Dr. Smith's observation recognizes a truth that can provide a foundation from which both "religionists" and "spiritualists" can conduct mutual exploration. It recognizes that there is mutual interest in *liberation*, but erects yellow flags around two important issues, namely, that *liberation needs direction* in order to avoid *empty headedness* and that *direction needs liberation* to avoid a *doctrinaire traditionalism*.

For me, this insight puts the oil where the squeak is! Under the weighty limitations of institutional religion, I yearn for liberation, but liberation that has some direction; yet, the kind of direction needed is *liberated* direction. Diana Butler Bass' book, *Christianity After Religion: The End of Church and the Birth of a New Spiritual Awakening*, is a scholarly exploration of the new possibilities that await us if we are committed to the validity of a liberated traditional faith and to the merits of those who are finding fresh paths to meaningful and faithful living.

Her title is revealing: It speaks of "Christianity *After* Religion...," suggesting the continuation of something substantive arising out of the ashes of "religion." The subtitle, "The End of Church and the *Birth of a New Spiritual Awakening*" emphasizes something beautiful coming to birth—as in the case of a butterfly—as the old cocoon begins to peel away.

I, along with some of you who read these pages, sometimes grow anxious about the dramatic change going on all around us. Obviously, at this juncture in the 21st century, things are not as they were in our youth. But, isn't that the nature of life as we know it? Isn't there at the base of existence a *dynamic* spirit that keeps us moving forward; not a *static* one that locks us in place to keep things the same?

At the heart of Bass' book is her focus upon four great periods of spiritual awakening. She indicates that a close look at the horizon will reveal the fourth of these is appearing and, like a breaking sunrise, is beginning to cast its warming rays. With this new awakening is what she calls "The Great Reversal" in which our previous "assumption that religious commitment begins when we assent to a body of organized doctrines" is being reversed: "Instead of believing, behaving, and belonging, we need to reverse the order to belonging (being in *community*), behaving (faith in *action*), and believing (from our experience with Christ and the community of faith, affirming God as the One in whom to place *trust*). And therein lies the difference between religion-as-institution and *religio* as a spiritually vital faith" (bracketed descriptions included with the quote are mine) 2

In this work, I have attempted to describe, in my own experience, the journey which has taken me forward toward spiritual freedom I was only beginning to imagine during those early years as I listened to the old sages, sitting around the pot-bellied stove on Saturday morning; talking religion. That experience agitated my young spirit to the point of triggering a journey that continues to introduce me to the phenomenal ways in which a deeper experience with God bathes my life in a profound sense of freedom.

I am so pleased that you have shared my journey by reading this book. I hope the process has been rewarding to you.

I want to leave you with this quote from Diana Bass with which I deeply resonate:

"In a very real way, we are all religious immigrants now, faithful people who have—willingly or unwillingly—left the old world for a new one, a place that exists largely in the hopeful risk taking of those seeking a meaningful way of life that offers peace and prosperity for all. This is especially true when it comes to faith. The old religious world is failing, but the Spirit is stirring anew. On the stage of awakening, I imagine Christians carrying high the cross, all the different varieties with their Bibles, prayer books, icons, and rosary beads; Jews holding the Torah; Muslims bearing the Qur'an; Buddhists with their Dharma wheel; Native peoples beating their drums; and so on, each group, cheering its own flag. But then, the reign of God shows itself, as promised in these ancient words from the prophet Isaiah:

In the days to come the mountain of the Lord's house

Shall be established on the highest of the mountains, and shall be raised above the hills; all the nations shall stream to it.

Many peoples shall come and say,' Come, let us go up to the mountain of the Lord, To the house of the God of Jacob; that he may teach us his ways, and that we may walk in his paths. 'For out of Zion shall go forth instruction and the word of the Lord

from Jerusalem. He shall judge between the nations, and shall arbitrate for many peoples; they shall beat their swords into plowshares, and their spears into pruning hooks; nation shall not lift up sword against nation, neither shall they learn war

*anymore (Isaiah 2:2-4—NRSV.)*3

END

NOTES

CHAPTER 2

1 Diana Butler Bass, *Grounded*, (San Francisco: Harper, 2015) p 36

2 Ibid, p 37

3 Ibid, p 37

4 Sally McFague, *The Body of God: An Ecological Theology* (Minneapolis, Augsburg Fortress, 1993) p. 37

5 Richard Rohr, *The Universal Christ* (London: Ashford Colour Press, 2019) p. 36 p.38

6 Ibid, pp. 40

CHAPTER 3

1 Wilfred Cantwell Smith, *The Meaning and End of Religion* (New York: Macmillan, 1962) p. 58

2 Diana Butler Bass, *Christianity After Religion* (New York: Harper One, 2012) p. 59 p. 62

3 Ibid, p. 61

4. Abraham Joshua Heschel, *God in Search of Man* (Farrar, Straus, Giroux 1955) p 64

5 John Buchanan, *Universal Feeling* (Ann Arbor: IMI Dissertation Service, 2007) pp. 66

6 Sharon Baker, *Razing Hell* (Louisville: John Knox Press, 2010), p.80

7 Richard Rohr, *The Universal Christ* (London: Ashford Colour Press, 2019) p. 103

8 Ibid, p. 99

9 Ibid, p. 100

10 Ibid, p. 104

11 Rob Bell, *Love Wins* (San Francisco: Harper One, 2011) p. 113

CONCLUSION

1 *A Magazine for Friends and Alumni of Johnson University,* "OnMission" By L. Thomas Smith, Jr (Knoxville 2018) p. 117

2 Diana Butler Bass, *Christianity After Religion*, (New York: Harper One, 2012) p. 119

3 Ibid, pp 120

Journeying Forward Toward Spiritual Freedom

FORM FOR RECORDING YOUR RESPONSES

Chapter 1: The Early Years

CHAPTER 2: A Fresh Approach to Faithful Living

CHAPTER 3: Some Implications of the Loving Lifestyle

CONCLUSION:

www.ingramcontent.com/pod-product-compliance
Lightning Source LLC
Chambersburg PA
CBHW071456070526
44578CB00001B/357